MONKEYS UP A TREE

10/9/18

To Nancy

Best Wishes

Rosemary

MONKEYS UP A TREE

A MEMOIR OF
AN AFRICAN CHILDHOOD

Rosemary Gordon

Columbus, Ohio

Monkeys up a Tree: A Memoir of an African Childhood

Published by Gatekeeper Press
2167 Stringtown Rd, Suite 109
Columbus, OH 43123-2989
www.GatekeeperPress.com

ISBN: 9781642371123
eISBN: 9781642371178

Printed in the United States of America

CONTENTS

For my daughters: Shellan and Candi.
Always my most ardent admirers and the bearers
of seven wonderful gifts: my grandchildren.
I love you.

Special Thanks to my brother Michael
for his contributions and memories.
To my writing teacher Linda Runyan,
you taught me so much.
To my writing buddies:
Molly, Susan, Janie and Irish for lending
me your ears, eyes and ideas.
To Susan FitzGerald, my sister-in-law, for
holding my nose to the grindstone and for
her unwavering faith in my writing.
To all my friends and relatives, thank you
for your constant encouragement.
To my editor, Alison Owings. Your
belief in Monkeys gave me the final
impetus to complete this memoir.

Africa is a place you have to leave before you realize how much you love it, and then there is no going back, back to the place you knew, that is, because it has changed and so have you.

—Rosemary Gordon 2012

AN INDEX TO FOREIGN WORDS

BAAS (Afrikaans) — boss

BAMBO (Chinyanja) — respectful address to a Malawian black male

BWANA (Chinyanja) — white man

BUSHVELDT (Afrikaans) — the bush

CHIPERONE (Chinyanja) — heavy mist and fog

CHONGOLOLO (Fanagalo) — millipede, also spelled Shongololo

DHOBI (Chinyanja) — a male person who does laundry

DONA (Chinyanja) — a white woman

EEI (Chinyanja) — no

E bloody ikona: E: (for Eei no in Chinyanja) — Ikona: (for no in Fanagalo) — throw a bloody in the middle and you have a: No way. Absolutely not.

FIGA (Fanagalo) — come

GALIMOTO (Chinyanja) — motorcar

GAVINE (Zulu) — illegal 100% proof liquor similar to Moonshine

IKONA (Fanagalo) — no

INDE (Chinyanja) — yes

INDABA (Fanagalo) — affair, discussion, news, information usually held with the headman of the kraal (village)

INDUNA (Fanagalo) — headman of the kraal

JAAPIES — what English speaking people call Afrikaners.

KAFFIR BEER — a beer made by fermenting maize

KAIA (Fanagalo) — house, usually a hut

KOPJE (Afrikaans) — a small hill

LAPA (Fanagalo) — here

MAYI (Chinyanja) — mother, respectful address to a white woman

MLONDA (Chinyanja) — night watchman

MUNT (Fanagalo) — a disrespectful name for blacks

MUSH (Fanagalo) — really nice, great

PICCANIN (Fanagalo) — small child, young child *

Piccanin, in my Africa, was not a derogatory, offensive word as is piccaninny in America.

In my experience picaninny was a word never used. In the language Fanagalo, both blacks and whites referred to each other's young children as piccanins.

The word piccanin, when used by ex-pats, was usually used with affection.

SJAMBOK (Afrikaans) — whip originally made from rhinoceros hide

SIKOMO (Chinyanja) — thank you

SIS (Afrikaans) — word used to express disgust

SUDZA (Shona tribe in Rhodesia) — a stiff porridge made out of ground maize rolled into a ball to dip in gravy

TSHETSHA (Fanagalo) — hurry

TSOTSI (Fanagalo) — hooligan, scoundrel

TUMUCH (Fanagalo) — a lot, too much

VOETSEK (Afrikaans) — bugger off

*Fanagalo is not an artificially-manufactured language like Esperanto. No learned professor sat down and invented it in a moment of inspiration! The fact that it is a vigorous language must be attributed mainly to two things:

1. It is more easily and speedily learned than any other language in the world.
2. It is a widely-spoken language, in constant use, filling a real need.

Fanagalo is a very much simplified version of Zulu, Xhosa and related languages, with adaptions of modern terms from English, Dutch and Afrikaans. It probably evolved in the Eastern Cape and Natal, and later Zimbabwe, during contacts between European settlers and African tribes, and it developed on diamond diggings, gold mines and farms to meet the urgent need for a common language that could easily be acquired by Zulus, Xhosas, Swazis, BaSothos, BoTswanas and Matabeles, and by the white men who employed them.

Excerpts from Fanagalo Phrase-Book Grammar Dictionary by J.D. Bold.

There are many different languages spoken in Southern Africa, Mozambique Namibia, Central Africa, and Malawi.

English, Afrikaans, Dutch, Zulu, Xhosa, Tsonga (Shangaan), Venda, SePendi, SeSvambo, Herero, SeTswana, Ovambo, Nama, Damara, German, Portuguese, Shona to name a few.

Fanagalo, spoken since pioneering days, is the bridge between these diverse languages. Fanagalo is taught on the various mines. It has even been used as a communication with Bushmen, of the Kalahari Desert, who speak with clicks and other strange noises. Fanagalo, most probably derived from "enza fana ga lo" which means "do it like this" or" kuluma (speak) fana ga lo (like this)

Fanagalo
Phrase-Book: Grammar Dictionary
By: J.D. Bold
Published by: J.L. van Schaik

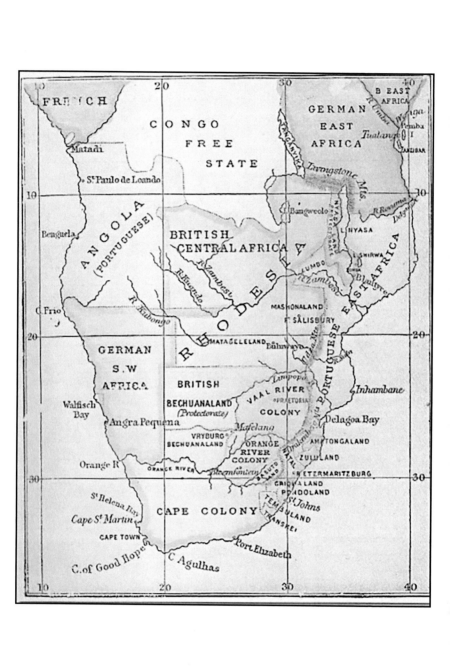

MY AFRICA: THE SMOKE THAT THUNDERED: MOSI-OA-TUNYA

Wildness is the nature of the place I was born, the savage and wonder-filled place where my siblings and I grew up. Our mother was a woman in Africa, a woman *of* Africa. She was as untamed and unpredictable as the animals in the bush, as funny and clever as a monkey, as brave as a lioness, as mean as a snake, as destructive to her family as an elephant is to trees. She was not a typical African mother. Oh no, a typical African mother attended and took close care of her children. How can you raise children with care when you raise so much hell, so much turmoil? When you root, then uproot?

My mother, part-time homemaker, part-time home wrecker, was as elusive as the pot of gold at the end of the ever-present rainbow in Victoria Falls, near where we lived for a time in what was then named Rhodesia. The natives on the Southern Rhodesian side of the falls, where we lived, call it Makulu Manzi

(Big Water) and on the Northern Rhodesian side they call it Mosi-oa-Tunya, (The Smoke that Thunders).

This "Big Water" was a place for desperate souls to plunge, a splendid, spectacular place to plummet to a chosen death. Time it right and your body would pass through the rainbow, the vibrant, arched rainbow with its pot of gold hidden in the spray, forever illusive. Do they scream, these souls, in terror or in exhilaration? The roar of the falls holds that secret forever.

My mother held no secrets, no matter how emphatically she promised she would. No, no secret was safe with her.

My mother was a woman who loved hard and fast. She gave of her love, but she was a Scorpio, with the sting of a scorpion when scorned. She was as generous, dangerous and violent as the land she lived in, and as paradoxical. She was my Africa, my smoke that thundered. I embark on this business of remembering for a need to understand why she did the things she did. Perhaps then I can finally forgive her.

And so I go digging.

BLACKWATER FEVER ORPHANS

My maternal grandmother, Flora MacDonald was eighteen when she and her family immigrated to Rhodesia from Australia in 1916. Traveling on the same ship to Durban, South Africa, was the Australian soprano Dame Clara Butt. Dame Clara had been booked for a singing tour of Europe, via South Africa. She heard Flora singing one day and was so impressed with her voice that she took her under her wing for the duration of the trip. She would have her lie flat on the poop deck and sing. This exercise, she said, would help throw her voice. Dame Clara encouraged Flora to seek a career on the stage and told her she should not waste her beautiful voice. That, however, was not meant to be, for soon after Flora's arrival in Rhodesia she met my grandfather, Harry Walker Richmond. *He* was not about to share her with the stage.

Harry Richmond had a lot of living under his belt by the time he married the beautiful Flora MacDonald. She was 20 and he was 34. Harry, besides being an engineer, was a pioneer of sorts, having left his home in Yorkshire, England in the late 1800's. He was an adventurer, a hard-drinking white hunter, a man's man, as men so often pictured themselves in the European colonies within Africa.

He had been called upon to work in the Congo to assist in the development and fulfillment of Cecil John Rhodes' dream of a "red line" (crossing boundaries) railroad from the Cape to Cairo. Due to geographical and political reasons the railroad was never completed.

By the time it was abandoned, Harry Richmond had fallen in love with Rhodesia, just as he had fallen in love with Flora, and he decided not to return to England. Instead, he took his young bride to a farm near the Nils Desperandum ("Do not Despair") Asbestos mine in Shabani, Southern Rhodesia, where he had obtained work. Here their three daughters, Pamela, (my mother, the oldest child), Patricia, and then Muriel were born.

The mine was large, the number of settlers small. Contrary to its name, there was much to despair. Living conditions were harsh, communications poor, and roads deplorable. A small school was set up in the mine and came under the supervision of a Miss Hines; this is where Pamela, Patricia and Muriel would attend class when they reached school age.

Perhaps it was Harry's drinking, perhaps it was because he went hunting for weeks on end and she was lonely, perhaps it was because of her suppressed dreams of becoming an opera singer, or perhaps it was because she was so young when she met him. Perhaps it was all these things that caused Flora to stray. But stray she did.

Pamela, who adored her father, told him that whenever he went hunting, her mother would visit the young man on the adjoining farm. One day Harry returned earlier than expected from a hunt and lay in wait for her on the path. He dragged her back by her long auburn hair, barricaded her in the house, and beat her brutally. When the bruising from that beating faded, she left Harry and her children, to move in with her lover. But she returned three months later, wracked with a disease known as blackwater fever. The writer Beryl Markham describes it well:

> * I don't know what the scientific term for blackwater is, but the name those who have lived in Africa call it is apt enough.
>
> A man can be riddled with Malaria for years on end, with its chills and its fevers and its nightmares, but, if one day he sees that the water from his kidneys is black, he knows he will not leave that place again, wherever he is, or wherever he hoped to be.
>
> He knows that there will be days ahead, long tedious days, which have no real beginning, or end. They run together into night and out of it without changing colour, or sound, or meaning. He will lie in his bed feeling the minutes and the hours pass through his body like an endless ribbon of pain because time becomes pain then. Light and darkness become pain: all his senses exist only to receive it, to transmit

to his mind again and again, with ceaseless repetition, the simple fact that now he is dying."

*West with the Night by
Beryl Markham (1942)

Harry, distraught, guarded Flora's room where she lay in a delirium. He clutched his shotgun across his chest and would not allow her lover or her children to see her. Flora was dying.

Unaware of her surroundings, she sang haunting arias in the last three days of her fever. Her beloved Alsatian dog, Sheba, did not come off the nearby kopje for those days; she did not eat or drink but howled continuously. She knew her mistress was dying.

There was nothing to be done for Flora but for the fiendish blackwater fever to take her. Finally, it did. After she died, Harry still did not put down his gun, but guarded her body and her room for three more days. She was only 34 years old.

Pamela, 13, Patricia 12, and Muriel (known as Mu Mu), 9, essentially lost both parents the day blackwater fever took their mother. Harry Richmond, always a heavy drinker, now drank more than ever. His Flora was gone, and so was his will to live. He packed his daughters up and sent them to a small boarding school, twenty miles away. An African farm hand delivered them in a wagon, trunks and all, to the school, where they would live for the next two years. Harry, meanwhile, moved four hundred miles away, to Northern Rhodesia.

Upon arrival at the school, the girls' trunks were deposited with the housemother. Pamela, in the role as the eldest, and now the surrogate mother, instructed the farm hand to "Wait here until I say you can go." She presented herself to the Head Mistress, who, after introductions and a little chat, said what Pamela heard as, "Okay Pamela, you must return to your farm now."

Striding back to the wagon, Pamela told the farm hand to collect their trunks. They would not be staying there after all. She then marched into the housemother's office, where her sisters waited for her. "Come on Patty, come on Mu Mu, we have to go back to our farm. They don't want us at this school."

"Why, Pammy?" Patty asked, running after her sister.

"I don't know Patty. The Head Mistress said we must go back to our farm."

The housemother, when she understood what had happened, explained the misheard difference between farm and form. She told them that the Head Mistress wanted the sisters to go their classroom, their form. And so, the farm hand was duly dispatched back to the all-but-abandoned farm, minus his grieving cargo.

The three sisters, from left to right,
Muriel (Mu Mu), Pamela and Patricia

Harry Richmond died two years after Flora. Pamela always said he died of a broken heart. He actually died from heart failure, which, I guess, could be called a broken heart. His children were told that he had pleaded for water at the end, but for some reason could not have it. Nurses dampened his lips with a wet sponge.

The night of his death, Muriel was discovered sleep-walking in her nightdress, on the wall of the balcony outside her dorm, three stories up, with a glass of water in her outstretched arm. "Here Daddy, here's your water," she was saying, "I've got your water, Daddy." The housemother gently coerced her off the balcony, leading her back to bed.

The three little orphans, who were left with no money to pay for their boarding school, were sent to live with paternal aunts in Bulawayo, approximately 200 miles away. The girls' lack of money to pay for anything made them realize almost immediately that they were not welcome, nor were they ever treated with the same love or concern as their cousins.

My mother Pamela remembered the plaintive conversations. "Can't we have cream and golden syrup on our porridge too?"

"No, it's too expensive. You can have sugar or salt on your porridge."

"That's not very fair," replied Pamela, always the outspoken one.

"It's not very fair that your father left you with no money either, and I have to look after you. I'm not going to deprive my children because of you lot."

Three crushed, shamed faces, stared back at this ugly, unkind auntie.

So, sugar it was, but nothing could sweeten that bitter porridge. Is it any wonder that my mother Pamela looked for love wherever she could find it? She fell pregnant at sixteen. The father of her unborn child was a married man, who would remain unidentified. He was never spoken of, at least not that my siblings or I ever heard.

Patty, always her sister's keeper, was not about to let her Pammy's baby be born illegitimate. In those days, that bore a terrible stigma for both mother and baby.

Patty ambushed Gerry Fitzgerald, a man who had been courting her, Patty. She grabbed him by the arm, outside his place of work at knock-off time. With tears running down her cheeks, she begged. "Gerry, please, please will you marry Pammy? Please, Gerry. Pammy's baby has to have a father, a name."

Gerry Fitzgerald, a kind man, agreed. A marriage license was duly obtained, a ceremony performed. Days later, Pamela was taken to the Bulawayo Maternity Hospital. Un-bastardized in the nick of time, Peter Fitzgerald was born four months after my mother's seventeenth birthday. On his birth certificate was written the father's name: Gerald Rupert Fitzgerald.

Legitimate.

Gerry Fitzgerald took his new wife and son to Filabusi, 75 miles south of Bulawayo, where he had found employment on the Fred Mine, the largest gold mine in Rhodesia. As was customary, the family was allotted a company house. Mom nested. She loved babies, and my brother Michael was conceived two years after they moved there. I was born a year after Michael. Geraldine and Avril came along three years and four years after Michael. Years later, in a rare moment of candor, Dad would tell me that it was Aunt Patty he was in love with. And Patty? I think she too lamented her sacrifice. She would sometimes tell me that she really should have married Gerry.

Retrospectively Dad and Aunt Patty were far better suited to each other, as were Mom and Uncle Ernie. How life messes with us — or do we mess with life?

Did Pamela love Gerry? From all accounts, she was certainly grateful to him for providing a roof for her and her son. And she was content for a while. But a wildness, a restlessness, lurked in the shadows of the domesticity Gerry created. Soon he would come to bore her. He was not enough for her. As we would learn, nothing was ever enough for her. Including us, her children.

I have read that there is near-universal scientific acceptance of the fact that the mind is capable of avoiding conscious recall of traumatic experiences. In searching the dark corridors of my mind, occasionally a door opens, allowing me to retrieve a snippet, an incident, but alas, there are still so many closed doors.

This is where the digging in those gardens of my past gets more difficult. How to make sense of the senseless, to find the why? I find a lot of weeds, but I find flowers, too, smiling at me through the sunshine on their petals. They seem to say, *look at me, too.* We are here amongst these weeds. See? We've survived in this wilderness, this wildness, and so can you.

I tried. And in many ways, I did survive. And I still do.

A BUMPY ROAD AND A BLUE BABY

It was a bumpy road, the road that led me to my birth on December 10, 1941. A bumpy, dusty, dirt road, full of potholes, ruts and broken-up strips of tarmac. A road that started from the gold mine in Filabusi and ended in Bulawayo, Southern Rhodesia. Mom had been placed on an old mattress in the bed of Dad's 1930's lorry. While I bumped about in Mom's belly, that lorry rattled around on that bumpy road traversing dry riverbeds, fallen trees and circling dislodged boulders. It also stopped often for the crossing or sauntering of elephants, giraffe, warthogs or troops of baboons. It was a road that challenged you, argued with you, demanded negotiation, or so I was told, at least by Mom. "That dreadful bumpy road," Mom would tell me, "is why you were born like that. Born a blue baby, yellow with jaundice. You almost died, you know. You did."

But I survived. I rose like the yellow African sun, the gold from the mine, the Fred Mine.

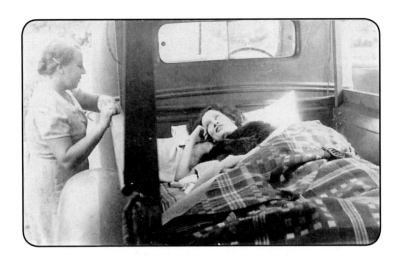

Mom was made comfortable on a
mattress in the back of Dad's lorry for the
journey to the hospital for my birth.

It was a puzzlement, a confounding curiosity to
me as a child, this business of blue and yellow. A yellow blue baby! How can that be? Was I yellow with
blue stripes like a zebra? Or blue with yellow spots like
a leopard? Mom never explained exactly. I think perhaps I was blue with yellow bumps, from that "dreadful bumpy road." Or, maybe yellow and blue, both. But
wouldn't that make me a green baby? I knew yellow
and blue made green because once I mixed my watercolours and painted my doll and she was green.

When I finally learned to string words together,
I would tell the kids I met, "I'm a blue baby, you
know."

"No, you're not. You are not blue."

"Yes, I am, I'm blue. But sometimes I'm yellow
too."

Yellow as the golden nuggets in that mine, the gold that resides deep within its bowels, where men go in to find the precious, the valuable.

I go now into my own mine, my very own mind, where a tarantula lurks. My first memory is of that tarantula, a dark, ugly tarantula, as ugly as any spider can be. That black, body-shuddering spider, bigger than a saucer, is raised up on all of its eight hairy legs on Daddy's pillow.

The baby that is me shakes the wooden slats of her crib. Rattle. Rattle. Rattle. "Da-da-da." Rattle. Point.

The scary, hairy tarantula inches close, closer, even closer to Daddy's face. Daddy has seen it now, out the corner of his eye. I know he has. Keeping his head very still, he carefully rolls up his Rhodesian Herald newspaper. Slowly, ever so slowly, he lifts the paper.

WHAM. WHAM.

The ugly black spider lies there now, flat on the pillow. Limp and twisted.

The tarantula's bite, though painful, is not poisonous to humans, unless you are allergic to it. Nobody knew that then, not in those days. "Rosebud saved my life," Daddy would say. Daddy always called me Rosebud. I was very brave, he said.

Not a chicken.

Not a coward.

Not yellow.

GOOSEBERRIES AND A STRANGE HOUSE

But I was not so brave a few years later on a dark night when I went with Mommy to a strange house. "Wait outside," she told me.

Why had she gone inside? Whose house was this? I didn't know it at all, this house, but I did know that Mommy should not be in it.

I stand on the dirt path in front of this strange house that swallowed Mommy up. What was she doing in there? It had been a long time. Now the sun has gone. The darkness wrapped itself all around me like a prickly, itchy blanket. I'm itchy, itchy inside my tummy, where I can't scratch. There are gooseberry bushes on the side of this path and bogeymen in the shadows. I know there are bogeymen because I see their hands, their heads, sometimes even their eyes.

Fast as I can, I pluck the gooseberries off the bush, one by one, and stuff them into my mouth.

Pluck. Peel. Stuff. Pluck. Peel. Stuff.

The yellow ones with the brown papery jackets, they're the sweet ones. Peel. Stuff. Peel. Stuff. And then I vomit. The vomit squirts out my mouth, my nose. Lumps of gooseberries, once sweet, now bitter, are down my dress, on my bare feet, in the dirt.

Mom bursts out the door, grabs my arm, yanks it. "Come on, Rosebud." She pulls me behind her, stumbling along on the uneven path. My mouth tastes so bad. My nose smells of vomit. My tummy… Oh. It hurts.

At last we are home.

Bang. Bang. Bang Mommy pounds on the front door. "Open the door, open this damn door," she shouts.

The damn door opens, and Daddy stands there in his rumpled blue-striped pajamas. His bed-messy hair sticks out all over. His eyes blink. "Where have you been?" he asks, sleep in his voice, "It's so late."

Smack. The sound of her slap makes me jump and I start to wail.

"Don't you dare question *me* you bastard!" Mommy says through clenched teeth.Slap, one side. Slap, the other side.

Daddy's fine brown hair lifts, shivers in the air, then, plops down on his head just over his eye. Mommy's angry red hands stay there, on Daddy's cheeks, both cheeks.

"Daddy, please don't hit Mommy. Please, please, Daddy, don't hit her. Don't hit Mommy." I cling to Daddy's pajama legs, tight, tighter. Snot is dripping off my lips. "Pleaaaase, Daddy."

Daddy looks down at me. His eyes are sad, so very sad that this child would think he was going to hit her mother. This child that is me. This child of indeterminate age, this child who loves her Daddy, is sad too.

The years between that strange house, that stranger's house, and a school without a name are lost. Lost is such a bad word, isn't it? It's a hateful word, a word that doesn't feel good in your mouth.

"You what? You lost a shoe?"

Found, is a much better word, especially when you can say; "Look, Mommy, I found it, I found my shoe!"

But I often didn't find what I lost. The biggest thing I kept losing was my dad.

I lost those years from the strange house to a school with no name. Those years from our house in Filabusi to another house, two or three hundred miles away, in Salisbury. Those years are gone, blank, unfound.

Dad was there at first, in Salisbury, and then he was gone too. Lost.

FAT RAINDROPS: I FEEL SAFE WHEN IT RAINS

You know when the rain is coming because of the thunder. BOOM, BOOM, across the heavens it resounds while dark clouds gather. An electric bolt of lightning zigs tsssssssssssssss . . . zags, tsssssssst . . . zigs, zigging, zagging tsssssssst-down, down...CRACK. Crack. Sharp, dangerous, cracks.

Fat raindrops bounce off the thirsty earth, at first sending little whirling dust clouds up like mini tornadoes. Then they soak the patiently waiting earth. The earth waits for this nourishment from above to nurture all the hidden life buried in the parched dirt below.

The big rain, the fat rain, pounds and clatters down on our corrugated tin roof in the house where we now live in Salisbury. If it's a Saturday, the din blots out the sound of the beating drums coming from the compound where the black workers and their families live. Those Saturday night drums frighten me because I know, with those drums, comes much drinking of kaffir beer and the alcoholic drink, gavine and this usually means there will be fights, and stabbings too. Once I saw a black man stumbling down the road with a knife stuck in his back, just the handle showing. And once when we opened our back door a black man was sitting on the doorstep with an axe in his head, blood running down his face. He just sat there holding the handle of the axe up, waiting quietly for us to wake up and help him. These are the things that frighten me when I hear the drums.

Mom says the troublemakers are the tsotsis (criminals/thugs) and that it's the gavine that makes them crazy. Gavine is illegal. Mom says it is made out of sugar cane and it's a hundred percent alcohol.

The police are always raiding compounds looking for the gavine the natives brew in empty petrol tins, which they then bury in the ground. When the police find it, they pour it out on the earth – to much sighing and head shaking from the drinkers.

You have to be careful in electric storms. People who find shelter under trees are sometimes struck dead by lightning. The tree is a conduit, we are told, and we should never, ever stand under one in a lightning storm, or near a window with bare feet, especially on wet cement floors.

After the rains, leaves are greener, watering holes fuller, and the air is filled with the smell of wet earth.

I love the rain, for all these reasons but especially because it makes me feel safe. Tsotsis don't go out hooliganing in a storm, or so I believe.

A BIG BLACK BIRD ON A MOTORBIKE AND FISHY FINGERS

There were men. Strange men. Men who came and left, others who stayed awhile. You hated them all, because you knew as long as they were with Mom, Dad wouldn't be.

Where is Dad? He is not in this house of ours in Salisbury. Lost, he is. His lorry is not parked in the yard, but a shiny black motorbike is. Its name spelt out on it. NORTON.

Mom is always bursting out of doors. On this particular summer day, she bursts out of the front door of our house, her red hair on fire, standing out really, like hundreds of springy chongololo legs. The chongololo is a giant centipede. Mom is mad. As mad as a wet hen, she would have said. Well this hot day, she is as wet and as mad as any hen would be after several gins and tonics. I stop my skipping and watch her with a thumping heart. What's the matter? Why is she so mad?

Mom unscrews the petrol cap on the tank of that motorbike in our yard, screaming, "Bastard, you bastard! You're not going anywhere."

Frantically she lights matches from the Lion matchbox in her shaking hands, tossing them one by one into the tank. The flames die as soon as the match leaves her hand, or breaks in two. She continues to drop them in the tank anyway.

"Bastard!" Strike. "Bastard!" Strike.

The "Bastard" now bursts out the door, the same door Mom had burst out of a moment ago. He is shoving his arms through the long sleeves of a black shirt. It flaps at his sides like the wings of a big black bird. He flies to his motorbike, snatches the cap from Mom's hand, screws it back on the petrol tank, straddles his bike, jump starts it, turns it around. He did not say a word.

Black Bird's motorbike revs, roars, skids, sending dust and stones pelting. They sting your bare legs, these stones, like bullets from a pellet gun. Out the driveway the Black Bird goes, winging its way in a cloud of dust down the road. Feathers ruffled.

"Good riddance to bad rubbish." Mom screams.

"Go, rubbish," you scream, hopping up and down in glee. Maybe Dad will come home now.

They had faces, these men, but you don't remember them. You remember other things about them though, like their shirts, their hands, and their fingers.

You never did know who that blackbird on a Norton motorbike was. Nor do you know this other man who sits beside you and Mom on the small brown couch in the lounge, across from Dad's favourite wingback chair. It is a blue chair with green and gold leaves. It has been empty for a long time, empty and forlorn without Dad. If anyone sits on it I tell him or her, "That's my Dad's chair." And they move.

37

Now squashed together on this couch, Mom and you and him, this stranger, like three sardines in a tin. Momma Sardine, Baby Sardine and Fishy Sardine, so fishy he makes you wriggle.

"She has your fingers, you know," Mom says with teary eyes as she reaches for fish man's hand. Turning it over, palm side up, she pinches the puffiness of each of his fingers, close to the palm.

"Look," she says, taking your hand now, pinching your puffiness. "Just like yours. Just like your fingers."

You squirm. Who can he be, sardine-fishman? And why do you have his fingers? You don't want his fingers. You want your own fingers or mom's fingers or dad's fingers.

Your heart pinches. Please let it rain. You want to hear fat raindrops on the iron roof. And that Sardine Man and his fish fingers can go, go back into the ditch water to be washed down the drain.

"Come wi the wind an gang wi the watter" my great Aunt Polly would say in her Scottish accent. This fishy man came with the wind now you want him to go with the water.

It does rain, but not with fat raindrops. It rains with skinny raindrops and the sun shines bright. You run outside and twirl and twist, with your face up to the sun. The skinny raindrops softly touch your cheeks, your closed eyelids, and your bare, outstretched arms.

"It's a monkey's wedding! A monkey's wedding!" you squeal and shout to anyone, because everyone in Africa knows that monkeys get married when the sun shines and it rains at the same time.

Where he came from, this man with your fingers, and where he has gone now you have no idea, but you know there is something very shameful, something you can't quite put your finger on about him. But you do know whatever it is, it's not good for you or Dad. You go to bed with an achy, muddled up heart, too afraid to ask Mom about him, too afraid of what she might tell you. It's better to just forget about him, push him into a black hole, where you put things you don't want to think about. He stays there for a while.

HONEST POLIO

"Honest is as honest does," Mom always says. I think I'm honest. I try to tell the truth straight out. I do, that is, until that day that I didn't, that day when honest flew right out the window. Up and away it went, out the school window, across the schoolyard, into the bush and there was nothing I could do to stop it.

It all started with Jesus' food.

We gathered in a group, sitting in a circle on the grass in the playground of that school with no name. Brenda, Sonja, Gail, me and some other girls, eating our lunch. There was no butter for my sandwich that morning so the red mixed fruit jam had soaked into the bread, making it all sticky, wet and pink. Boys swagger around us, showing off, bothering us. They pull Brenda's plaits.

"I made you look. I made you poop I made you kiss the kaffir cook."

"It's not nice to say that," Brenda tells them.

We are not allowed to say kaffir, ever. Except when we say kaffir dog or kaffir sheeting or kaffir pots. Kaffir is a bad name to call a black person.

"Do me a favour, lick my bum and tell me the flavour," they sing back.

"Uuuuuuh, that's rude." We all squeal, sucking in our collective breaths.

"Stupid boys, They're so stupid, don't listen to them," someone pipes up.

"Do you want a date?" Gail asks me. Offering a jar of dates from her lunch box.

"No thanks, I hate dates."

"UHHHH." All of them now, boys and girls, suck in their breaths, looking at me this time. They, flick, and snap their fingers. Eyes big, mouths open.

"She hates Jesus's food." Those snapping fingers stop, and point at me. They get up, Gail, Sonja, Brenda and the other girls, walk away from me, looking over their shoulders, whispering, twittering.

Are dates Jesus' food?

The next day Billy Simons brings a model aeroplane to school. I want it, want it so badly, that plane, for my brothers, Peter and Michael. They will love it. They will love me too for getting it for them. "Gee thanks, Rosebud," they might say. I steal it from Billy's cubbyhole in the hall while no one is around. At least I thought no one was around. I hide it in my desk.

In the classroom, Billy raises his hand, shaking it waving it. Flapping really. "Teacher! Teacher! Teacher!"

"Goodness me! What is it, Billy?"

"Rosemary stole my aeroplane. It's in her desk. She stole it. I saw her."

"I did not."

"Yes, you did."

"No, I didn't."

"Okay, okay. Rosemary, did you take Billy's aeroplane?"

"No, Miss Atwell."

"Are you sure? Absolutely sure, Rosemary?"

I want to run out of the classroom, I want to run and run and run but I can't move. Pins and needles shoot into my head. I can feel them coming from all the eyes that are looking at me. Perhaps I can follow the truth and catch it, but I can't. It's too late for that.

Miss Atwell is beside me now. She knows. I know she knows.

"I haven't got it," I whisper.

"Well then, open your desk. Open it and show Billy that you haven't got it."

I lift the lid of my desk. The lid, quite strangely, feels as heavy as lead, and there it is, in all its sinful glory. It looks bigger than I remember. It fills my desk. It fills my head. My ears are two burning coals.

"Now give it back to Billy, Rosemary, at once, and apologize. Apologize to Billy."

My coals are glowing and so are my cheeks as I make my way over to Billy's desk with the aeroplane in my hot hand.

"Sorreeee." I mumble, my eyes on the floor.

"You lied. You're a liar, Rosemary."

I did, I lied. I sit in that lie, in the playground all through lunch break. All by myself hunched over on the steps.

"She's a thief," the kids say as they pass me on those steps.

"And a liar."

"*And* she hates Jesus' food."

Back in the classroom I squirm so much that I get all tangled up in my desk and the chair that's attached to it. One of my arms is caught between the rungs of the chair back and my feet are wrapped and jammed around the wooden slats under my chair. Stuck from squirming. Miss Atwell has to come over to untangle me.

I HATE THIS SCHOOL. I HATE GAIL. I HATE SONJA. I HATE BRENDA. I HATE DATES. I HATE ME.

I don't hate Jesus or God. But maybe God is punishing me for being a thief. Or maybe for hating Jesus's food. Because now, after six months of being tangled in that lie, I cannot get out of bed. I'm burning. I hurt all over, especially my left arm.

Am I going to die for my sins? I have heard about people dying. It can't be very nice to die, because when someone dies people cry, and then you don't see the person again, the person that died, that is. You see the person who cried. You see their puffy eyes and soggy, twisted up, handkerchiefs. No, I don't want to die.

"She has a high temperature, Doctor, and she complains of a terrible pain in her left arm."

Doctor Pretorius looks at Mom and says "Hmmmm."

I don't like that hmmmmm. This must be really bad, whatever it is I have, because everyone whispers now and Mom cries. I hear all of this, the muffled voices, from my bed in Mom's bedroom.

"What's wrong with Rosebud?"

"Shhh, Geraldine, she is sick, very, very sick. She has polio."

Polio! Now I know what that is. I have seen people who had polio. They're in wheelchairs, all twisted up and their mouths hang open, dribbling spit.

"He had polio, poor fellow," people would whisper behind their hands. I think I would rather die than be twisted in a wheelchair.

But I don't die and I'm only a little twisted. "She's lucky," people say. "She only had a mild dose."

So lucky I am that I only have a curvature of the spine. So lucky that I have a right foot that is one size smaller than the left foot. So lucky that I have to wear a built-up shoe because I'm now three quarters of an inch shorter on that side, my right side, where all my wrongs have come to sit. I have to go see a physical therapist who tries to make me straight again. I stand with heavy, weighted suitcases. Up, down. Up, down. Up, down. The one suitcase is heavier than the other and my arm gets tired. Up, Down, Up, Down.

All this business with the suitcases is because they don't want me to get more twisted than I already am.

The Rhodesian Herald had reported an outbreak of polio and everyone was asked to come to the clinics and take a teaspoon of the vaccine, a pink liquid. A lot of natives won't take that vaccine because they think it's a plot by the white man to sterilize them. You see a lot of twisted black people. Some white ones as well.

I don't want polio. I think of the aeroplane I stole. I will never take anything that doesn't belong to me, not ever again, I promise God.

Mom is always taking things that don't belong to her. All over our house there are things that used to belong to other people. Ashtrays that have Limbe Golf Club or Zomba Club or Monkey Bay Hotel on them, glasses and beer mugs too. She also has a nice silver tray and silver salt and pepper shakers with a coat of arms and The Shire Highlands Hotel etched on them. The best of all is a soft white dressing gown that tells you it's the "Property of the Meikles Hotel." Well, it's Mom's property now.

Mom says they want you to take these things, all these things with other people's names on them that used to belong to them but belong to us now. "It's advertising for them," she says.

"You'll get polio, Mom," I warn her.

TWISTED SECRET AND A TRAIN GOING

"A crookit stick will thraw a crookit shadow"

What I have learnt is that some people are twisted, not in their bodies but in their minds. They show you a friendly face, a kind face, in front of your mother. You don't know, not yet, that some people have another face, a hidden, ugly one. No one told you to look behind a friendly face for the real face, the twisted one.

You are so innocent about those two faces, of such duplicity, until that night you somehow end up sleeping in the double bed in Mom's room.

Your head feels stuffed full of cotton wool as you struggle up through layers of sleep. What is it? What is this hard thing on your back? It has a beat, a pulse. Then there are hands. Hands that move all over you, stroke your side, your hip.

"No, what . . .? What are you doing?" You push the hands away.

"Shhhh! Shhh! Don't wake your mother."

Where is your mother? Where is she? Snoring and gurgling she is, across the room on that small bed against the wall, on her back, her mouth wide open.

Why are you in her bed, this double bed?

"Stop it!"

"Shhh. Shhh. Relax, you'll wake your mother and she'll be mad. You know what she's like when she's mad."

The blankets fly up and into the air as you fling them off and scramble out of that bed. You run to your room, the one you share with Geraldine. You jump into your bed. Your heart thumps. Thump, thump. You lie as still as a mouse frozen in the path of a cobra. Wait. Wait. Wait.

He comes to your bed, Henry, Mom's boyfriend, does. Just as you knew he would. He comes pushing into your bed, pushing you against the cold brick wall. Squish. No room. No room for two on this bed. He touches you… down there.

"No, no, stop it. Stop it!"

"Rosebud, why are you crying, what's the matter?" Geraldine's frightened five-year-old voice reaches you from the other side of the dark room.

"Nothing, Deany, nothing. Go back to sleep. Go back to sleep." You are the big nine-year old sister, but you are frightened too.

He lifts you up and off the bed. He carries you into the bathroom that's between your bedroom and Mom's bedroom. *Click.* He locks the door. He has no clothes on. He sits on the edge of the bath, his thing sticking up, straight up, between his legs. You have never seen one before, not like that, all swollen and blue, but you know what it is.

He grabs your head and pushes it down. Down. Down. Down. And out. Out, out, out, you go. Blackness now. Gone.

47

You don't tell anyone. You keep this secret inside you, rolling it like a dung beetle rolls its load. A shiny brown scarab, that beetle is, about the size of a big toe. With its front legs on the ground, it pushes and rolls its ball with its back legs. The ball gets bigger and bigger, as it gathers more and more dung.

You are that beetle now, rolling up all the dung around you, pushing it into a deep, black hole.

You are also a Grey-Go-Away-bird with its loud warnings of: go-away, go-away, go-away. Flitting from branch to branch. In a tither, a tizzy, a tizzytither. Its bright pink gape squawking: GO-AWAY! Go-Away! It comes back though, that bad memory, it sneaks in on arms, on hands, on fingers. Go-away Blackbird. Go-away Sardine. Go-away Henry.

And now, we are to-go-away.

Thoughts of Henry gone for now, overshadowed by the excitement of a holiday. I'm happy because we are going on a train to visit Aunt Patty in Bulawayo: Mom, Geraldine, Avril and me. I'm extra happy because Mom told us that she has broken up with Henry. Yay! I think this is why we are going to stay with Aunt Patty for a fortnight, to get away.

We board the WHITES ONLY car on Rhodesian Railways. We have a compartment all to ourselves. The train pulls out of the station in Salisbury, chug-chugging in its effort to gather speed down the tracks.

"I baggies the top bunk." I shout.

"I want the top bunk," Geraldine whines.

"Oh, for crying in a bucket," Mom says, "There are two top bunks, you can each have one."

Chug-chug. Chug-chug. The whistle blows. Brakes screech. The chug-chug gets slower and slower each time we pull into or out of one station after another. All four of us hang out the window to wave at the piccanins who run alongside of the train, hands out, sweet, beaming little faces with dry snot making number-eleven marks from their noses to their lips.

"Sweets, Missus. Money, Missus." We have two big tins of Quality Street sweets, one for Aunt Patty and one to share with the piccanins. We throw handfuls of sweets out the window at every station. The children smile as they scramble and jostle for our sweets littering the platform.

There is much coming and going at these stations, much bumping and banging as passengers push and shove to get on and off the train. Native women with huge bundles balanced on their heads, babies tied to their backs with bright-coloured blankets, lugging chickens in baskets or stuffed into O.K. Bazaars's plastic shopping bags, just their squawky little heads sticking out. The men walk in front, not carrying anything, except perhaps a briefcase and a knobkerrie (a type of club). This is how it is in Africa. The men always walk ahead with their knobkerries to fend off snakes on the path in the bundu. But there are no snakes on the platform and still the women carry all their things.

Mom nips into the station bar for a beer at these stops. "What will we do if Mommy misses the train?" Geraldine asks.

"She won't, Deany, she won't," I reassure her, not believing myself because I am sure she will miss the train this time. She doesn't. She always makes it back on the third whistle warning. Each time, three anxious faces, six saucer eyes, greet her.

"We thought you were going to miss the train," Geraldine and I chime as one.

"Don't be silly."

At one of these stops, instead of going into the bar, Mom buys fruit from a vendor on the platform. Back in our compartment, she scrubs out the steel wash-hand basin and makes a large fruit salad with paw paws, bananas, apples, oranges and granadillas. We all dig in, sharing a single spoon.

Mom says we cannot afford to eat in the dining car. I wish we could though, just once, like the other white people do.

Knock. Knock. "Tickets please."

We drop our spoon in the basin, slam the lid down, sit back, pick up our books, and pretend to be reading.

When the conductor leaves, we go back to our fruit salad and looking out the window. The dry bush veldt, dotted with flat-topped, fever trees, rolls by. They are acacia trees, actually, but are called fever trees because, at one time, they were thought to cause malaria, until people found out that it was the mosquito. The thorns of these acacia trees are so long and sharp, they were used by the Boer settlers as sewing needles. Unfriendly thorns they are to you and me, but the giraffe has learnt how to get around them. Sometimes you will pass one trimming the treetops. Lazily it turns its head to watch you flash by.

Another kind of tree catches my eye. "Look, bao-babs!" I yell, "See? They are upside-down trees. The roots are at the top instead of in the ground. They are prehistoric, you know," I state with authority. "They're the dinosaurs of trees."

We keep seeing claw-like flowers, yellow and red, that change to a deep ruby, edged with gold. "Those are flame lilies," Mom tells us, "They're Rhodesia's national flower." There are lots of them.

There are lots of guinea fowl too, darting this way, that way, and all about. They look like black balls with small white polka dots. Bouncing balls. Balls with turquoise necks topped with red combs. Dotty little things running helter-skelter as though they're lost. Perhaps they too have lost their Daddy. I think my Dad is working on the mine and sending Mom money. I secretly hope he will come back to us now that Henry is gone.

Everywhere we look there are zebras. "Mom, are zebras black with white stripes or white with black stripes?"

Mom looks at me with an empty face and shakes her head. "Goodness me, I don't know. Could be either way, I guess. But I do know that every zebra has unique stripes all his own, like our fingerprints. Amazing, isn't it?"

Everything is amazing about this train journey.

"That's an Ndebele village," Mom informs us as we pass thatched huts within sandy walls that are painted with geometric designs, big and bold. Yellow, orange, blue, and white all outlined in black. Startling colour in this sea of brown. Women sit, backs to the walls, beading or grinding maize, piccanins playing all around their outstretched legs. Skinny yellow-eyed kaffir dogs sniff the ground for scraps of food, digging the hard earth. Digging instead of dogging. So intent on scavenging, they don't even look up as we pass.

We look up and out, this time to see tall jacaranda trees, dripping with lavender flowers. You know you are approaching a town when you see them and their enormous lavender bouffant tops with thick circles of lavender carpets underneath. Flamboyant trees too, with bright red flowers. The flamboyant is a tree originally from Madagascar that were planted in the tropics as street trees. Some people say Mom is flamboyant, as though that was not a nice thing to be. But I think it is. And then the din and clatter and clutter as the train chugs into another station.

Knock. Knock.

"Here's your bedding," the conductor says, bringing us our sheets, blankets and pillows. Rhodesian Rail ways Rhodesian Rail ways Rhodesian Rail ways, woven in a straight blue line across the top of the white cotton sheets. The prickly brown blanket also says it belongs to RhodesianRailways. We have to give the conductor money for using this bedding. Mom says she feels like taking it all with her tomorrow when we get to Bulawayo. "We've paid for them, after all."

She doesn't take them, but she does take a towel that also tells you it belongs to the RhodesianRailways. It belongs to us now.

As does sleep, sleep, which comes quickly, easily on that top bunk, between those starched white sheets. There will be no twisting and turning between these sheets. No need for the Go-Away bird this night. Out the train window he'd flown with Henry hanging onto his tail.

THE NAKED SINGER
WITH A GOLDEN S

On the train going back home, after a fortnight of forgetting, of playing cops and robbers, of building forts in old anthills with my cousins in Bulawayo, my heart pinches and squeezes remembering, in time with the rhythm of the clickity-clack of the train. I am worried because I heard Mom tell Aunt Patty that she had talked to Henry.

I negotiate with God, the way children often do. Please, please, please, God, don't let Henry be at the station. I promise I will say my prayers every single night. Just please, don't let Henry be there.

He's there.

How could you, God?

On the platform, packages in his arms, stands Henry, wearing a rugby jersey draped around his shoulders, the sleeves tied together on his chest. A stupid smile on his face.

He hands Geraldine a box. He hands Avril a box. Then he holds a large box out for me. Everything is rushing around inside me, rushing from my head to my feet, my feet, which are stuck to the platform. They are so heavy I can't lift them. What is the matter with them? They're not feet anymore. They are bricks at the end of my shivery legs. I can barely breathe. I stare at him while my inside-me races and shakes.

Geraldine and Avril rip open their presents. Mom is looking at me as if to say: Come on Rosebud, be nice. But I can't be nice. I hate, hate, hate, him. Mom told me she wasn't going to see him again, never again. She lied. I didn't really believe she would stay away from Henry. But she could have told me he would be at the station. She didn't, though, and here I am, held hostage by my feet on a train station platform. There are sleeping forms under blankets everywhere. I would like to get under a blanket too.

One minute? Five minutes? Ten minutes?

Then the platform that had been holding my bricks glued to it, lets them go. I turn and get into Henry's old brown jalopy. I do not take his box. He is left standing there, offering his box to no one. His face is red, almost as red as mine in the back seat of his beat-up car.

From the front seat, Mom looks over her shoulder at me. "What on earth is the matter with you, Rosebud?"

She knows. Mom knows what the matter is. She knows I hate him. She doesn't know why, but I know she knows I hate him.

Staring out the window, my eyes see nothing. A hot, burning ball sits in my chest. I fight back tears. I don't want him to see me cry. I don't want him to see this wobbling, this shaking, of me.

Back home, I run into my bedroom, slam the door, fall on my face on my bed, and cry. The tears I have held back as hard as I could soak into the pillow.

Mom has opened that big cardboard box that Henry tried to give me, taking out the sewing machine inside. It's in her hands now, naked, as naked as Henry was that night in the bathroom, that night just a few weeks ago which feels like a lifetime away.

Mom sits on the edge of my bed next to me. She touches my shoulder. "Look what Henry bought for you. Isn't it sweet of him darling? Isn't it?"

"I don't want it."

"Why not? Don't be silly, Rosebud. You told me you wanted one so badly."

"Not anymore. I don't want one anymore."

I peek. It's beautiful, that sewing machine. Shiny black with gold scrolls and a big golden S. It's just what I had wanted for so long to make clothes for my doll. Mom sees me peeking.

"Here, Rosebud," she pushes it towards me, "take it. Please, please. You'll hurt Henry's feelings if you don't."

"I don't care, I don't want it." My hands clenched, nails digging into my palms, snot and tears dropping off my chin, "I don't want it."

"Well, you're being very unkind. I didn't know you were such an unkind little girl."

That sewing machine disappeared and so did Henry. They disappeared from the house but not from my head. Where he went or why, I don't know. All I know is that I felt a huge relief. My secret could be guarded.

I couldn't tell Mom why I didn't want that Singer or why I hated Henry so much. I couldn't, I just couldn't tell her. I couldn't tell anyone, not for a long, long time, not for about seven or eight years. And then I told Aunt Patty.

Dad, who had disappeared, came back again, in a letter. It was in 1950, just after Henry finally vanished. Dad had applied for a position advertised in the *Rhodesian Herald*. The job was to run a borehole drilling company in Nyasaland owned by Sid and Rose Bell. They hired him, and he was to stay with the Bells family until a company house was rehabbed for him. Michael was with him and Peter was in boarding school in Salisbury. Dad wrote to Mom proposing some terms for the two of them to get back together.

The first pages are missing.

> ......a really clean start, with no fear that things will come out at a later date as they are bound to. There is so much that depends on your answer, so don't be afraid my dear, it won't make any difference now. It's only that I have got to know everything before we start life anew, to avoid all the suspicion and unpleasantness and we will be able to face everybody together, not separately well wont fear (sic), tell me everything and make me love you again, as I want to more than anything else.

> It's six in the morning (Sunday). We are all busy, going down to Chirambe, we spent the whole day there yesterday, Sid, Rose, Mac, Stan and Mickey on the house. Stan is Rose's

son up on leave from Byo. He has spent most of it on the house, a grand chap, thinks the world of Mickey. They were both on the roof, putting shingles on (it's going to take 18,000, about to cover it). Anyway they both sit up there singing away at the top of their voices, banging away for all they're worth and Mickey blinking as hard as he can, you know how he does when anybody bangs. Anyway there is only the bathroom side left. Then that completes the roof. Mac and Sid put two ceilings in yesterday so that leaves four ceilings to do and painting, anyway we have broken the back of it, I put in the concrete for the French drain and am going to brick it over today. It's ever so lovely there, Rose has been planting that fine lawn grass in the front, rose trees and other things. She is trying to make it nice for you so that you will be happy there and I think you will. I hope so anyway.

I wish I could bring myself to have an affair with some of these women here; it would put us on the same basis then.

I want you to delay your departure as long as possible so that I can have the house ready for you.

I would not want you to stay in one of the hotels here, keep away from temptation and everything will be fine.

All my love to you and the kids

Yrs. As ever

Gerry

Now there would be another train and more stations. Some we would stop at, the ones that had passengers waiting. Others we would slowly glide by, eventually stopping at Limbe, where Dad and Michael (Mickey) are to meet us, Mom, Peter, Geraldine, Avril and me. We are to stay with the Bell's too, until our house is ready.

This train is taking us on this new journey, a journey of hope. It's going to be a "new beginning, a fresh start," Mom tells us. But the fresh start has to wait for a while, until the almost-ready-house is ready. In the meantime, we are to stay at Chigamula Estates with the Bells. Mom says this will be an adventure and she seems excited.

For us to go forward together, though, Mom has to stop drinking. She has to climb back on the wagon, the one she'd fallen off in Salisbury, before Dad's letter came. She made that climb, and now on this journey she is our funny, loving, energetic mother again.

When we get to Limbe, Dad and Michael are waiting for us on the platform. Both of them have big, fat, smiles on their faces. We wait on the platform as our suitcases and boxes are off loaded. I watch Mom. Is she happy? Will she be nice to Dad? She is quietly watching him. They're both still. So are we. then Dad moves to her, puts his arm around her shoulder and she laughs, looks up at him, and says, "Phew, what a long hot journey, that was, Gerry. Take me to a bath, I need to soak in a hot bath." She kisses his cheek and the worry that has been in my stomach for the longest time goes away. Dad hugs us all and my heart swells with happiness and love. Everything will be all right if only Mom stays on the wagon.

CHIGAMULA AND THE BELLS.

All Dad's energy has to go into finishing our house. Then, finally, everything will be as it should be. Well almost, because, it's not actually our house, it belongs to Aunt Rose. She is the real owner. In addition to Chirambe, she owns Chigamula Estates, where she and Uncle Sid live in their big house. She also has a dairy, a sawmill business, tobacco and drying barns, a Tung nut grove and a borehole drilling company, where Dad works, where Dad finds water with his branch. He had lived with Aunt Rose and Uncle Sid for a few months before we'd arrived. So now we stay here, too, with Aunt Rose and Uncle Sid, until our house is ready. I like Uncle Sid, everyone likes Uncle Sid but I'm not so sure about Aunt Rose. Sometimes I like her, when she's not bossy.

Aunt Rose and Uncle Sid Bell are not really our aunt and uncle. We just call them that. All children call them that, and Aunt Rose calls all children her "bairns." She is particularly besotted, Mom said, with Avril. "Look," she would say, of Avril, "She has my walk." This would make Mom mad and she'd respond with: "She came from *my* loins, Rose." Slitting her eyes.

Aunt Rose is fluent in Chinyanja, the native language of Nyasaland. And when she is on the warpath, which she always seemed to be, she instills fear in the hearts of all her workers. She has fourteen servants in the house, and many more in the tobacco fields, sawmill and dairy. For the house there is Cookie, the cook, his three helpers, four houseboys by day and waiters by night, a dhobi (launderer) a m'londa, (night watchman), and four gardeners.

She marches everywhere she goes, her big bunch of keys jingling on a large ring at her waist. Everything is kept under lock and key. Ingredients for the day's meals carefully measured out from the locked larder each morning. She says she trusts Cookie. I think to myself, *but not enough to give him a key to the larder.*

Everyone gets very busy pretending to do busy stuff when they see her coming.

Aunt Rose is 5' 2" tall. Small on top, she balloons out at the bottom with huge hips, thighs, tree stump legs and thick ankles. Her thick ankles show she is from common stock, Mom says. Thunder Thighs we call her, when we don't call her The Sergeant Major. Peter and Michael say she could jump-start a Dakota aeroplane. Her jaw protrudes with an under-bite. She looks just like the porcelain bulldog that sits on the side table in her lounge. To everyone around her, except Mom, she is: *she who must be obeyed.*

Dad goes to his office or out on surveys every day. Most of the time he drops Mom off at Chirambe to garden and supervise work on our future house.

Aunt Rose's home at Chigamula is an orderly place. Beds are turned down with hot water bottles placed between starched white sheets, to warm your feet on chilly nights. It's a place of mosquito nets hanging from the ceiling and tucked under mattresses. A place of floors polished daily by houseboys on hands and knees. The smell of paraffin wax mingling with aromas from the kitchen and Cookie in the kitchen. Cookie always in the kitchen. Everyone knows it's his kitchen. But not his larder.

Every afternoon, before high tea, the march takes place. The feet and fingers march. Aunt Rose's two-inch heels click and clack around the polished wooden floors, taking her eyes and fingers to the bookshelves, the top of desks, the windowsills, searching for undusted surfaces. Woe betide those whose rags and feather dusters missed these places. At six o'clock, cocktails are wheeled into the lounge on the drink trolley and then dinner at seven thirty, on the dot, bairns's hands and faces all washed and hair all combed.

The dinner bell rings. Cookie must not be kept waiting. We take our seats at the table, Aunt Rose at the head, Uncle Sid at the tail, and the rest of us in between. Four waiters line the walls behind our chairs, their stiff white uniforms and white gloves, spotless. Red fezzes on their heads, tassels all to one side, all the same side. They stand, backs to the wall, visible yet invisible.

"Michael, you didn't comb your hair."

"Sorry Aunt Rose, I forgot."

Tsk. Tsk. A tongue clicking on the roof of her mouth, a gentle shake of her head, a little smile that says you are forgiven, but only this time.

The first course is wheeled in on a trolley by one of the kitchen boys. The waiters leave their walls to place steaming bowls of chicken soup before each one of us.

"May we start?" we children ask in unison.

"You may," says Aunt Rose.

Clink. Clank. Clink. Spoons beat a tune on the sides of the china bowls. Slurp. Slurp. We tilt the bowls away as we've been taught to do. Finished. With a look and a nod, Aunt Rose signals the removal of our empty bowls.

That smell, that delicious smell that has been coming from the kitchen all afternoon is wheeled in. Roast beef and Yorkshire pudding, Cookie makes the best Yorkshire pudding in the whole world, soft in the middle and crispy and brown around the edges from the pan juices. There is never enough for me.

Uncle Sid carves the beef, placing slices together with the Yorkshire pudding on our hot, always hot, dinner plates. Once again, the waiters leave the walls and circle the table, this time with serving dishes of roasted potatoes and vegetables. There they are again, those hard-to-eat, fresh-from-the-garden peas that we are never allowed to shovel with our forks.

Aunt Rose tells us of the time she was giving a very fancy dinner party and Cookie was instructed on roasting a whole suckling pig to be garnished with roasted apples and a whole apple in the pig's open mouth. She had demonstrated by taking an apple to her open mouth, "like this," she says.

First courses were consumed, and the waiter walks in holding a large platter with the beautifully roasted pig. In the waiter's mouth, stretching it to bursting point is an apple! Even Mom laughs.

Aunt Rose looks at me and says, "Rosemary, I saw you outside today without your pith helmet and shoes."

Of course you did, you with the eyes in the back of your head.

"I forgot, Aunt Rose."

"Well, you know the saying 'only mad dogs and Englishmen go out in the midday sun.' It's dangerous, you know, Rosemary, to be out in the sun without your pith helmet, and I'm sure you don't want more putzis in your feet. Do you?"

Mom never makes us wear those stupid hats. "No Aunt Rose, I don't. I'll try to remember."

No one would want a putzi. They are so disgusting. You can get a putzi from wearing clothing that has not been ironed; the putzi fly lays eggs in clothes hanging outside on the line to dry. Upon contact with human skin, the eggs hatch. The larvae burrow into the skin and develop into fully-grown maggots. They eventually come to a head like a boil. You have to put Vaseline on it so that the maggot can't breathe. Then you push on your skin, and a fat, white, maggot pops out, leaving a hole you can put the end of a pencil in. I had one in my heel, from wearing socks that had not been ironed. UGH.

"Michael did you go to the dairy today?"

"Yes, Aunt Rose, I . . . "

"I did, Aunt Rose, I did."

"Geraldine, if you insist on interrupting your brother, please say excuse me." Mom gives Dad one of her looks the one that says, *these are my children.* Dad looks away.

"Sorry, Aunt Rose, sorry."

Schnicker-cough-shnorkel. Peas spray out from Michael's mouth, bounce on the table, roll to a stop.

"Yes, Geraldine, don't interrupt me"

Uncle Sid grins.

Geraldine giggles.

Mom says "Michael!'"

The waiters' eyes twinkle.

The last course is wheeled in. A large bowl of orange coloured granadilla pulp, a bowl of thick fresh yellow cream from the dairy and a platter of cheese and crackers.

"Sikomo, Bambo, tell Cookie we will have coffee in the lounge."

"Inde, Dona."

In the lounge, Dad and Uncle Sid listen to the news on the radio. Mom darns socks. And we play rummy with Aunt Rose. Mom interrupts the news to ask Dad, "Gerry, when will the house be. . .?"

Aunt Rose interrupts Mom, "Gerry, Mr. Pillay called, he needs a borehole."

Uh! Oh! Mom gets that look in her eyes, that narrow look, the one that means trouble. Her lips get thin making a red gash on her white face.

Who will Dad answer?

"Pam," he says, "The house should be ready in a week."

Phew!

Mom thinks that Aunt Rose is in love with Dad. I think so too, because the other night when Mom and Dad were going out to a dinner-dance, Aunt Rose threw a tantrum and smashed up all her own 78 rpm records, the bits scattering all over the floor. She was screaming and crying. I don't know why, but it didn't do any good. Mom and Dad left. We kids had to stay with Aunt Rose's tantrum.

Finally, our togetherness house is ready. "About bloody time," Mom snaps, "I was ready to kill that woman. How and why Sid puts up with her, I'll never know. He's far too good for her."

Yes, just in bloody time, I also think. Given any more time and that bloody woman would have ambushed our father.

We remove ourselves, all seven of us, from Chigamula and go forward into Chirambe, Chirambe is about two miles away. Mom thinks it's not far enough away from Rose Bell.

Forward to our fresh start as a family and probably the happiest time of my childhood.

CHIRAMBE, THE TOGETHERNESS HOUSE

It's a large brick house, this new house of togetherness with a verandah running the length of three sides. There's no electric power. Sixpence, our houseboy, lights kerosene lamps every evening. Water for our baths is heated on a wood stove and all our drinking water is filtered. A large, screen fronted box, draped with wet hessian (burlap) is our refrigerator. There is a very big bathroom off one end of the verandah and Peter and Michael's room is off the other end, making brackets for the house.

Mom's trunk carrying all her unfulfilled dreams and ambitions (she wanted to be a film star, you see, and everyone said she looks like Katherine Hepburn. When they said that she would suck her cheeks in) arrives at Chirambe, shipped from Salisbury. A few new stickers adorn the outside: THIS SIDE UP: FRAGILE. Residents of that trunk, pasted to its walls and under the lid are Ava Gardner, Greta Garbo, Cary Grant, Rita Hayworth, Errol Flynn, Greer Garson, Bogey and Bacall. All Moms' idols, living right there, in her trunk with the mothballs. Her prisoners. Their glamour, the glamour she so yearned for in her own life, is hers momentarily, whenever she lifts the lid.

Mom finds some red and white gingham fabric buried within this trunk, just enough to make curtains for the kitchen. She goes shopping for more material and finds lovely blue sari fabric at the Indian Trading store. This she uses to make curtains for the lounge.

When she has finished the curtains, she gets busy sewing for everyone. Pins line her clenched lips, a tape measure over her shoulder, and with scissors in hand, she snips, pins and measures as she tackles a new piece of fabric with a fever pitch. Soon the recipient of this outfit would be on a chair while she drapes, cuts, tacks and tucks. Pinning sanitary towels in just the right place for shoulder pads. Sanitary shoulders.

Mom could finish a dress in three to four hours. Dad's shirts and trousers would take her a few days as there were pockets to be lined, collars reinforced, waist bands and flies inserted, and button holes sewn by hand. The heavy cast-iron iron rests on the hot stove. The ironing board also rests, close to her elbow, with a sheet wrapped around its torso to hold the disgorging batting in place. A mummified ironing board.

Some projects, newspaper patterns pinned to cut out pieces of material, were abandoned and relegated to the trunk, to be finished later. There they would languish for years, the pins rusting and the newspaper yellowing.

Each time that trunk is opened for a viewing, an aura of mothball fumes rises and shimmers in the atmosphere.

"Won't this make a lovely skirt?" Mom enthuses, displaying her latest fabric, holding it to her waist, creating folds and drapes. Back it goes into the trunk, this well-travelled trunk that moved with her wherever she went. And she went a lot. But for now, she is here at Chirambe with all kinds of good intentions.

We are finally a family, all together again, and the house is coming together too. It's a full home, a home full. Mom is madly nesting. She arranges and rearranges the lounge furniture. She moves Dad's chair just as he gets comfortable with its new position. He is good-natured about it, even though he's a creature of habit.

"As soon as I get used to my chair where it is, Pam moves it." he says to anyone visiting.

Mom cooks our favourite meals. She makes the very best dumplings, we tell her. That is, I tell her, because dumplings are my favourite things along with Yorkshire pudding, to eat. One dumpling night at dinner Michael points his finger to something behind me and asks.

"What's that?"

"What?" I turn my head.

"I made you look...Ha.Ha."

My head spins but I knew before I looked back to my plate that I had been tricked.

My plate, where my treasured dumpling had sat, saved as the best for last, is now empty. With an unbelievable sense of loss, for I know there are no more dumplings, I look from snickering Michael to Geraldine, whose cheeks, not the ones she is sitting on, the ones on her face, are puffed out like a monkey storing its nuts.

Her eyes laugh but her mouth cannot. If it did the dumpling would pop out. Instead her eyes pop out and her face gets red. I know she is already feeling bad. I think she should choke. She doesn't even like dumplings!

"Mom, Geraldine stole my dumpling, my whole dumpling. Look, Mom, it's in her mouth."

"Geraldine, why did you do that? You know there are no more dumplings. That's mean."

I never, ever take my eyes off my dumplings again.

Mom cans guavas and makes guava jam. Jars and jars of these line the shelves in the pantry. There are hundreds of guava trees on the estate, and we like to climb them. We soon get to know which guavas to eat and which ones have worms.

Others eat these wormy guavas, though we don't see them. We see their poop, in little piles here and there. Little piccanins' poop, we figure, full of guava pips.

Mom makes pumpkin fritters, sprinkled with cinnamon, brown sugar and a squeeze or two of lemon juice. She makes banana fritters too.

Dad comes home from work and retires to his ever-moving chair after dinner where he listens to the BBC World News on his battery radio. He loves to listen to the news. He occasionally listened to the local Chinyanja station because it amused him. I love to see him sitting there in that chair. Found.

One morning Mom notices that Dad's radio is not beside his chair. She asks Sixpence where it is.

"Oh Dona, that radio, he not working, I think the Bwana has taken him to the shop."

"Really, Sixpence? It was working last night."

"The Dona, she did not hear that radio only speak Chinyanja last night? Me think the Bwana take it to the shop so that it can speak English again."

Mom laughs and laughs and when she tells Dad later he laughs. Of course, they don't do this in front of Sixpence, for they don't want him to lose face. Face is important to proud servants trying to learn the odd ways of the white man.

We are not allowed in Peter and Michael's bedroom, Geraldine and me. Why we wonder, can't we go in there? They come into our bedroom. What have they got in there, anyway?

"Come in," Peter says one day; he and Michael are lying on their beds on opposite sides of the room. Very relaxed they are with hands under their heads, sunny smiles on their faces.

"Go on, you can come in."

Hopping, skipping, we run into their room. Flip. Crash. We didn't see the wire Peter and Michael strung across the room to trip us up. We should have known, that "come in" was far too friendly.

But I don't learn. I'm gullible, Mom says. Just like the day Peter gave me a leaf to eat. "Mmmmm!" This is sooo good" he said smacking his lips "Mmmm, here take a bite, Rosebud." He held out that large green elephant leaf with a bite-size piece missing, the piece he was chewing, "Try it Rosebud."

I took it, that huge leaf the size of an elephant's ear, and bit into it. I always believed them, my brothers, because they were my heroes.

YIKES!!!! My mouth cringed, my lips puckered, my throat slammed shut, then opened just enough to let a squeak escape. Peter's eyes grew wide. He looked scared. Him looking scared made me scared. My eyes bulged. My hand found my throat.

"Spit it out! SPIT IT OUT!" Peter screamed as he squashed my cheeks with his hands, "SPIT." I spat and spat and spat. Did that strange strangled sound come from me, from my throat? Peter's finger swept the inside of my mouth and came out with green mush on it, a swamp finger.

"Did you swallow any?" he shouted, as though he hadn't told me to eat it.

"No. My throat wouldn't let me." My voice was mine again. Peter didn't look so scared now. He even chuckled.

"Sorry Rosebud, I didn't know it would do that."

"But you were eating it." I cried.

"No, no I wasn't Rosebud, I was pretending to."

"Dad, Mom," I screamed, "Peter made me eat the elephant's ear."

"Peter," Mom yelled, "the elephant ear plant is very, very poisonous. You are lucky it didn't kill her. Jesus wept and mother cried, don't do these things, Peter."

Dad was not amused either. Nor was I. I felt like smacking Peter's mouth, but as always, I soon forgave him.

Mom says I'm an easy target because I am so gullible, I always fall for their tricks. I don't really mind that they do these things though, not really, because I'm just happy we are all here in this togetherness house. Doing naughty things here with us is better than them doing good things somewhere else. Lost.

A REAL MAN DOESN'T SIT DOWN TO PIDDLE.

When we saw a cloud of dust spiraling up from the dirt road approaching our house, we'd all yell, "Aunt Rose is coming, Aunt Rose is coming." Then we'd scramble down the guava trees and make a mad dash for our pith helmets and shoes.

Into our kitchen, which she still thinks of as her kitchen, she marches, keys jangling. She lifts the pot lid of whatever Mom has cooking on the stove and proclaims, "Gerry likes his stew with potatoes," or "He likes the way I make such and such."

"I've been married to Gerry for thirteen years, Rose. I know what he likes and doesn't like," Mom says, steam coming out of her flared nostrils.

Later she complains to Dad. "Pam why do you let her get to you?" he says. "We have to put up with her for now. I work for her. It won't always be this way. When we get on our feet, we'll get a place of our own."

"She makes my blood boil when she walks into my kitchen and lifts the lids off my pots. Why don't you tell her to stay out of my kitchen, Gerry?"

"Let's not cause any ill feelings, Pam. Ignore her. She'll get the message."

"She's in love with you. That's the trouble. Sid knows. He's not blind."

"Okay, let's drop this, it's almost Easter. I have to go to the Post Office. Would you like me to pick up a roast for tomorrow?"

Yes, yes, I think, let's talk about a roast. Let's talk about anything except Aunt Rose.

"Yes, a nice, beef rump roast will be good."

Dad returns from the Limbe Post Office with a large box addressed to Geraldine, Avril and me, "Who do you think sent this, Pam? There is no sender address?"

"Really? Perhaps there is a note inside. It's probably from Patty," Mom says handing us the box.

Oooooh, we never get boxes in the mail. In fact, we never get anything in the mail.

"What's inside, Mom?" we ask as we clamour around it.

"I don't know. Why don't you open it?"

What's inside that box are three more boxes, two small ones and one big one. The small boxes are for Geraldine and Avril. The big box is for me. The small boxes are filled with pieces of chocolate, broken pieces that were once thin Easter eggs. The big box has the most beautiful Easter egg I have ever seen. The shell has thick chocolate with pink, yellow and green hard icing sugar flowers, leaves and bunnies. It's not broken. It's for me. There is no note. I know it's not from Aunt Patty as there is nothing for Peter and Michael.

"Who is it from, Mom?"

"I don't know." *I* think she does know.

"Why has Rosebud got the best Easter egg?"

"I don't know, Geraldine, maybe because she is the oldest."

"Ours are all broken."

"I know, I'm sorry. There's nothing I can do about it. The chocolate will still taste the same."

"It's not fair. It's not fair that she has the best one, with flowers and bunnies. We don't have flowers and bunnies."

I think it's not fair too and I think the chocolate eggs are from the fish man, that sardine who sat on our couch in Salisbury and I think I got the best Easter egg because I have puffy fingers just like his. My tummy flips and flops. These eggs scare me now.

Mom has fallen off the wagon because she has that off-the-wagon voice when I hear her say to Dad later that night, "You're not a real man. A real man doesn't *sit* on the toilet to piddle."

"Pam, don't start."

"Why do you sit when you piddle, anyway? Can't you stand like other men?"

I hate it when Mom says things like that. Dad's hurt would crawl under my skin, where I tried, as best I could, to wear it for him. I especially don't want him to know I heard such a shameful thing. I don't even want to know that my Dad piddles.

When she said things like that I knew it was her bad twin talking, because Mom is really two people: twins. A good, lovable twin and a bad nasty, twin. She is the bad twin when off the wagon and the good twin when she is back on it.

We circle her wagon and try to make her laugh. We try to be loving, lovable. More lovable than Gordon's London Dry Gin, and it works for a while.

Mom, the seamstress, sews us back together. Now, if the thread can hold the seams, the zips stay zipped, the buttons buttoned, then we can carry on being a family in this place of kids up trees, of rounder's or cricket and guava jam, of banana fritters, of radio listening at night, of darning socks, of pith helmets and yes please, and no thank you, and short back and sides and perms and fringes and ironed floral frocks. Yes, things will be just as they should be.

Mom turns her attention from piddling to chickens.

Standing in front of our togetherness house.
This is the only picture of us all together. Back:
Dad, Peter and Mom holding Avril. Below:
Michael, me, and Geraldine. We are all facing
the camera except Mom. She, I think, is looking
to see if the grass is greener "over there".

GREEN CHICKENS AND
DOUGLAS THE LEOPARD

Mom wants chickens. Decent chickens, she says, not those scrawny things they have in the native villages. She loves fresh eggs, especially the brown ones from the Rhode Island Reds. They have the extra orange yolks.

It was not easy raising chickens at Chirambe. It was a real challenge. To start, Mom has one hundred-day-old chicks airfreighted up from Salisbury. When they arrive, the fluffy, yellow, cheep-cheeping chickens are lovingly placed under the woodstove for warmth. The woodstove is in an open room off the kitchen where the night watchman rests between his patrols of the property. Everyone has a night watchman, needed or not, to guard his or her property from the rare thief.

"Now, mlonda, you look after my chickens."

"We! mayi."

"Don't put too much wood in the stove, understand?"

"Inde, Dona."

"Keep the fire low, like this. Okay Bambo?"

"Inde, Dona."

It's a loud scream, the sort of scream that sets your body shaking, especially when it comes in the middle of the night when you are sound asleep. My eyes pop open and I jump out of bed.

My shaky legs take me at a run to the boiler room, the Mlonda's room, off the verandah. That's where the scream came from. Mom is standing there in that room wearing her Meikles Hotel dressing gown, the one that used to belong to the spa. She is swinging a knobkerrie at the mlonda. Flames and sparks shoot out the gaping mouth of the woodstove. The light of them bounce around the walls of that small room, around Mom, around the terrified night watchman.

The mlonda, his arms covering his head, his bloodshot eyes bulging out of his black face, takes flight into the night, Mom after him still swinging that knobkerrie at his retreating back. Without a backward glance, his long dark coat flapping, his shoes crunching the gravel, he flees.

"Ayeeeeeeeee."

One hundred featherless, fluffy-less, skeletal chickens are on their backs, charred stick legs poking up in the air. "An extermination," Mom had called it.

"The bastard was snoring, can you believe it? SNORING! I hit him with his own knobkerrie. Look at my chickens," she says tears shining on her cheeks, "Just look at them."

"I'm sorry, Mom."

"Oh, my poor little chickens."

"Let's get some more," I say.

The night watchman was never seen again. For weeks Mom would say, with a chuckle, "That bugger is still running." I guess he was, because he never came back, not even for his wages. He knew he'd had a lucky escape from the wild, red-haired Dona with murder in her eyes and his own knobkerrie in her hands. Ee-Ee-Ee-Ee!

Into my nights come dreams of twisted burnt chickens.

Another one hundred chickens are sent for. The new chickens arrive together with a few hens and a second battle is about to begin, this time with hawks.

They would sit, those wily hawks, on high branches, with their striped tails and beady insolent eyes, challenging Mom: we have our dinner picked out. What are you going to do about it?

Mom, her eyes slit, her teeth clenched, would hiss, "Don't you dare touch my chickens, don't you *dare*."

Swish. Swoop, black feathers glinting in the sun. Talons spread, ready for the grab.

"Shooo! Shooo!" Mom screams.

Like a bolt of black lightning, a hawk zooms down and in to snatch a chicken right from under her nose. Off it soars, with the yellow, cheeping dot in its clutches. Squawk, squawk. The mother hen flaps her wings, runs in circles. Squaawwk, squawk, squawk. She is in such a flap.

Mom, with sad tears for her chicken and angry tears for the hawk runs onto the verandah to fetch my brother's pellet gun. With weapon in hand she stumbles over rocks, shrubs and squawking mother hens, shaking that gun in the air. "Leave my chickens alone! Do you hear me! Leave my chickens *alone* or I'll shoot you. I will. I'll shoot you."

This did not work. They were not intimidated. *Your gun does not scare us,* they seemed to screech from their lofty positions.

Next Mom came up with a brilliant idea. "I'll dye the chickens green? That will fox those bloody hawks."

She dips the chickens in green food dye. Now they're green puffballs, invisible in the grass. Sadly, this did not work either, since the mother hen, not colour-blind, set upon these green things chasing after her. She pecked them ferociously whenever they got too close to her. Mom had to wash the dye off.

Tiny, yellow, puffballs again. they chase after their mommy. She welcomes them back with much clucking, gathering them all under her wings. But it's to no avail. Those wicked hawks steal them, one by one, right from under her beak.

After that, with no chicks left, Mom took a broody hen and placed her on top of her eggs in a corner of the verandah. The next morning, all that is left of those eggs and the hen are a few sad feathers scattered here and there. Large paw prints form a path across our dusty verandah. That's when we knew that Douglas the Leopard had paid a visit.

Douglas, a marauding leopard, attacked calves and dogs and now he was taking hens off our verandah. Douglas became a constant worry to me. It was *me*, I knew it was me, he really wanted to rip apart, just as he'd done to that calf the other day at Chigamula. That poor calf with vivid red gouges on its body and flesh and skin hanging, as it lowed pathetically. The calf that had to be shot, "to put the poor thing out of its misery," Uncle Sid said.

It made me cry in my bed at night thinking of that calf.

The natives believed that Douglas the Leopard was actually their dead Chief Douglas, who had come back in the form of this leopard. For that reason, they would not hunt him.

Douglas came to my bedroom window one night. Scraaatch. Growl. Scraaatch. Geraldine and I, shaking, peep out. There right under our window are two big, bright, hungry eyes shining back at our peeping ones.

"Dad, Dad, Dad! Douglas is at our window!"

Dad opens our window, spots two giggling, two legged creatures running off into the black night with a torch and a paper bag. "It's Peter and Mickey." Dad whispers. He has a frown for us, to show he is not amused, but there is a small flickering smile on his lips for them. He tries to hide his smile. But it's too late, we have seen it.

"Go on, go back to bed girls. Sleep tight, don't let the bugs bite, if they do catch a few and we'll make an Irish stew." Dad always says that, every single night.

Still, we worry about Douglas. How could we go to the loo across the verandah? How could we, with Douglas in the shadows, ready to pounce on us? We know he's there, in the bushes, hungry for our flesh. We know he is waiting. We wait too, Geraldine and I, legs crossed. We wait until we can't wait any longer. Then we run, lickity-split across the verandah, wee-ing in our pants all the way.

Everyone says Douglas is getting far too brash. He has to be stopped before he attacks a child, they say. A white hunter is sent for. He flies up from Salisbury and amidst great hullabaloo and many ind-abas with the live chief, Douglas is eventually shot. Now we can go to the loo without worrying.

But there would be other terrors of the night.

Ants were just one of them. Black ants come to our beds one night. Thousands of ants. Crawling all over me. Nipping my eyelids, my lips, crawling up my nose, in my ears, around my neck. I scream, pant, slap at my face, tear and snatch at my pajamas. The crawling is under my skin now, in my tummy, in my hair. Geraldine starts to scream, and I know the ants are attacking her too. "Gerry," Mom yells, "run a bath, quickly. Rosebud and Geraldine are black with ants."

We have cold baths with Dettol in the water and our hair washed and still we feel them. "They're gone, they're gone," Mom tells us. We sleep in the living room shivering from the cold baths and shuddering from the ants. The next morning our room and the walls, inside and out, are sprayed with DDT and the iron legs of our beds are placed in tin cans of water. That war was won, one of the few.

Mom loses the chicken war. The fire, the hawks and Douglas won. She gives up on the chickens and Dad and us, one chiperone-enshrouded night when she jumps out of our bedroom window to go off with a man named Warren Cluff, tossing us, her other green chickens, here, there and everywhere. Like tennis balls on a court, we bounce.

Mom had met Warren Cluff at the bar in Shire Highlands Hotel in Limbe. She shouldn't even have been there, in that bar. She had snuck off while Dad was at work, just as she has snuck off now with Warren.

The chickens that had come home to roost had left in the talons of the hawks, in the jaws of Douglas and in the flames of that old woodstove. Mom had left too, like her mother all those years ago. She didn't come back. Dad takes us three girls to move back in with the Bells. I cry and cry and cry, for Mom. If I'm here at the Bells, who will look after Mom? Dad can't stand my crying any more. He takes me to Mom and then he files for custody of Geraldine and Avril. Peter, Michael and I are now with Mom. Geraldine would go to boarding school in Blantyre, Peter and Michael to boarding school in Salisbury, and I vaguely recall doing a home correspondence course.

IT REALLY IS TOO LATE AND A NEAR SUICIDE

Dad could find water where no one else could. He used a Y-shaped branch to find it. "Look, Rosebud," he would say when I went with him one day, "See how the stick is bending. See it? That means there is water, water right here. This is where I will drill."

Yes, Dad was a diviner. He could find water anywhere. But Mom, like water, was hard to hold on to. No matter how hard he tried, he couldn't find a way to hold onto her.

We had left that place of distant drums and dusty roads. That place where I loved to see Dad, sitting in his chair at night, listening to the BBC news. That place of candles, dinner bells and banana fritters. Of woodstoves and deep verandahs. Of climbing guava trees and tripping wires. Of night watchmen and knobkerries and fires and fireflies and bright stars and black nights. A magic, sometimes tragic place, of hooting owls and cunning hawks that had snatched Mom's baby chicks right from under her nose. "You don't scare us with your "Shoo – Shoo and wild red hair," they seemed to squawk.

That place where we were a real family for such a short while. And I hate Warren Cluff. I hate him with every fibre of my body for breaking up our family.

So now we are Dad-less again, but he is only half-lost this time, since at least we know where he is. He is back at Chigamula. Right back where Aunt Rose had always wanted him to be.

Mom is told by her solicitor that she must move out of Warren's house if she doesn't want to lose her children. And so, we move into a big old house Mom has found, way out in the bundu. Very isolated it is, with only one set of neighbours, Mr. and Mrs. Jones, within miles of us.

Mom opens a hairdressing salon in the Shire Highlands Hotel, the very place Dad did not want her to stay when we first arrived in Nyasaland, as his letter had stated: "Keep away from temptation." She and Warren fought a lot there because they were both tempted by the bar ten steps from the salon.

Dad comes to our house one day before he leaves again. I see him standing on the new verandah with Mom. He shifts his weight from one foot to the other. I hear him, too. "Pam, for the children's sake, please, let's try again. We can make it work, I know we can, if only you will stay away from the booze."

"No," Mom says, "It's too late, Gerry."

Dad's shoulders go down, his eyes fill up, he turns, walks to his lorry, drives away. I have never felt sadder. I want to run after him, hang onto his legs. Instead I run after Mom and hang onto her arm. "Mom, Mom, it's not too late, it's not. Please, please Mom, take Daddy back, we need him Mom, it's not too late."

She looks at me with her narrowed eyes, pulls her arm away, "What are *you* crying for? He's not even your father anyway."

Why does this hurt my chest so much? Why? I knew it, didn't I? Didn't I? Of course I did. It's that Sardine Man. He's my real Dad. I don't want him to be my Dad. I want my Dad, the one I love, to be my Dad. But that Dad had come today as my Dad and left as Mick's and Geraldine's and Avril's Dad. He was not mine anymore, not even as a pretend Dad. I could pretend that he was my Dad before. But now that Mom's words are hanging in the air, hanging over me in bed at night, hanging everywhere for any-one to see, there can be no more pretending.

Later that night, the night which had come at the end of that bad day that the words were strung up and out to dry, things got worse, much worse.

"I'm going to die! Your mother is going to die!" Peter, Michael and I fall over each other to get to her bedroom, to her screams.

She sits there on the edge of her bed, an empty pill bottle in her hand. She looks at us, her eyes more scared than I have ever seen before. We stare back with our scared fright, me, Peter and Michael.

"I swallowed them. I swallowed them all." Her chin sinks to her chest. Her eyes close. "WAKE UP, Mom! Stand up!"

Peter and Michael yank her up and try to walk her but she keeps falling asleep. They run to Mrs. Jones to ask her to call Doctor Antou. We don't have a phone, but the Joneses do.

When Doctor Antou and Mrs. Jones come, they drag Mom out to the verandah, holding her up on her legs. They walk her, up, down, up, down that verandah, pouring black coffee into her. The coffee dribbles down her chin.

Drops of blood fall. Drip. Drip. She's bleeding! Bleeding! Please, God, please don't let our mother die.

Doctor Antou and Mrs. Jones continue to walk her, talking to her all the time. Up, down, up, down for hours, or so it seemed, until she stopped falling asleep. Then they lead her back to bed. Mom doesn't die.

Doctor Antou tells her, "Mrs. Fitzgerald, I have to report an attempted suicide. It's a criminal offense, you know?"

Ohmygosh. Is Mom going to go to jail now?

"Please, Doctor Antou, please don't tell the police," we all bawl, "Please don't."

"Okay, okay. I won't report this. But Mrs. Fitzgerald, you have to promise me, promise you will never, ever, do this again."

"She won't, she won't," we answer for her. "We won't let her, Doctor Antou. We promise."

Now we really have to watch her, Mom, all the time. That's the new worry, the one that sits on my shoulders, knitted together there with all the other worries: the falling-off-the-wagon: the jump-ing-out-of windows: the men: now the suicide.

Everyone knows your business before you know it yourself, Mom would say. Well, everyone knew there was a new man in Mom's life. Even the two young black men who were sitting on the post office steps knew. They were discussing the antics of the Dona With The Red Hair, the Dona that was married to the Bwana who could find water with a stick. The Dona, that is now with the Bwana who sells tobacco, the Bwana with a very bad temper. Too much fighting that Dona and that tobacco Bwana, too much trouble, too much drinking.

Aunt Rose, on her way to collect her mail, paused to listen to this discussion of our family's troubles. They prattled on, those two, completely unaware that Aunt Rose could understand every word they were saying. Of course, Aunt Rose enjoyed repeating what she had heard. Even the Natives were talking about Pamela.

We almost lost Mom that night. Had she died Peter and I would have been real orphans and Michael, Geraldine and Avril would have been half-orphans.

I'm mad with Mom because she knows what it's like to be an orphan, so why would she try and make us orphans? But mostly I'm scared that she will try it again. Now suicide hangs over my bed.

This big old house is too isolated, Mom says, it's too lonely out here. We are going to move into Warren's house. His house is just outside Blantyre, it will be better for all of us. But the only thing is all of us aren't here. Geraldine and Avril aren't here. They're with Dad and that bitch, Rose Bell, at Chigamula.

My siblings were like ghosts in my childhood, sometimes revealing themselves in vignettes, only to disappear again. Where they went or why, mostly remains a mystery to me. Oh, how I loved them when they did appear.

THE KIDNAPPING AND MOM IS ON A ROOF

It's a house of turmoil, this house of Warren's. It is not a house of togetherness, it's a house divided. Geraldine and Avril are with Dad at Chigamula. Dad got temporary custody of them. Peter and Michael are sent to Churchill School in Salisbury. And me? Well, I'm here at Warren's house of confusion. I chose to be here, I had to watch mom. After all, Dad is not my real Dad. Surely he doesn't love me like his real children. And so, I am here with another hole in my heart.

Mom is as mad as a wet hen again. "That bitch is not going to have my children, Warren. They are *my* children. The only way she will get them is over my dead body."

I hope she remembers her body was nearly dead from those pills.

It's pitch black on the dirt road that is taking us, me, Mom and Warren, in Warren's blue Morris Minor, to Chigamula. The ruts of this road rattle the Morris. The Morris rattles me, every bone of me.

"Watch out for that bicycle, Warren! Jesus wept and mother cried! You nearly hit that man Warren, you nearly hit him," Mom shouts.

Hoot. Hoot. Hoot. Too late for the horn hooting, he's already behind us.

"God darn it," Warren growls while trying to keep the Morris on the road, "You can't see them at night in their dark clothes. Why they refuse to wear white at night, I don't know. It's for their own good, for Christ's sake."

Someone had written a letter to the newspaper to say that blacks should wear something white on the roads at night. That had caused an outcry of indignation.

I saw the man, just as I see him now, wobbling all over the place until he falls into the bushes with his bicycle and his basket full of chickens. I see all this from the back window of the Morris. "Why are we going to Chigamula?"

Warren turns the lights off, rolls the car to a stop.

"What are we doing Mom?"

"Be quiet, Rosebud."

"Why are you whispering? What are we doing here?"

"Shhhhhhhhhhh."

Mom jumps out the door of the Morris and is soon swallowed up by the night.

"Where is she going, Warren?"

"Don't worry, don't worry, she'll be back soon."

Soon is not soon enough for me, for my heart, which is beating so fast I can hardly stand it. "But why…?"

No answer from Warren.

We wait, Warren smoking and me anxiously staring out the back window, quite sure all hell is breaking loose.

Then I see her running towards us with Avril in her arms. "Go! Go! Go!" she yells, panting. She tosses a crying Avril into the back seat with me.

"Where is Geraldine?" I ask.

"Warren, go for God's sake! Get a move on, will you!"

"Mom, where's Geraldine? We can't leave Geraldine. We have to go back, we have to go back, Mom!"

"Warren, can't this bloody car go any faster? That bitch Rose, she's going to come after us. She will. I know it."

"Mom, we have to get Geraldine! We have to get her."

"Stop it, Rosebud. I can't take your crying any longer. Stop it. I couldn't get Geraldine, okay? They saw me climb out the window with Avril."

"Who saw you?"

"Do you know that bitch Rose dug a hole in the road Warren? A huge hole and if we had gone any closer we would have landed right in it,"

"Why did she do that? Why, Mom? Why?"

"She knew I would come for my children. She knew that we would probably have driven right into that hole. We wouldn't have seen it in the dark. The bitch."

Headlights shine into the back window behind my head. "Someone is coming, Mom! I think it's Aunt Rose's station wagon."

"She'll ram the car Warren! I know she will. Mark my words, she'll ram us."

"No, she bloody won't, she dare not," says Warren.

Aunt Rose's car stops, she blares her hooter, turns around, goes back. We get away unrammed.

We are nearly back at the house when it starts, the shaking. Warren's whole body shakes. His hands tap and bounce off the steering wheel. Sweat pours down his face. What is the matter with him?

"Warren, pull over, pull over now. Stop the car," Mom tells him.

Warren pulls over and we sit there until his shaking stops. Nobody says a word about it and I'm confused and frightened, which makes me hold Avril tightly to my chest.

We get away with only one of my sisters and I'm so mad at Mom. I want Geraldine with us, but I also don't want to take her away from Dad, I don't want him to be lonely. But I don't want Geraldine to think we don't want her. Why is it so hard to keep us all together?

The next day Mom is hanging up washing, I stare at a funny-looking thing she has just pegged onto the line. "What is that?"

"It's a jock strap."

"What is a jock strap? What's it for."

"Never mind."

But I do mind. I know it has something to do with Warren, who seems, in the light of this odd thing, even weirder to me now. "Mom, why was Warren shaking last night?"

"Shell shock," she says "from the war. His best friend's head was blown off right next to him. He has lots of medals for bravery, you know."

"Oh.... Well, it is scary when he shakes." I still don't like him, brave or not. "I hate him Mom."

"Oh, come on, Rosebud, he is really a very kind, caring man."

"He's not kind Mom."

"He loves me."

So does Dad, I think to myself, and Dad doesn't hit you. Warren hits her when they fight. She hits Warren too, usually with her handbag.

We have Avril now and Aunt Rose is suing Mom for trespassing and breaking and entering, and Dad has Geraldine, but he wants custody of Avril too. We may have to give her back if the court says we have to. Mom says she will kill "that bitch first." There is going to be another fight for Peter and Michael, she says. What about me? I think. Is no one going to fight for me?

"We have to pick Peter and Michael up from Luchenza today, because I just know Gerry will be at the Limbe station to meet them," Mom tells Warren.

Peter and Michael are coming up from Salisbury on the train for the holidays. When we get to Luchenza, they are standing on the platform in their Churchill uniforms and so is Dad.

"You're coming with me boys," Dad tells them.

"Over my dead body," Mom says.

"They're coming with me. You underestimated me, didn't you, Gerry? You thought you could out-smart me, didn't you?"

The thing is Mom did think she could out-smart Dad by coming here, to Luchenza, the stop before Limbe.

"Pam, I think the boys should come to me."

"Who do you want to go with?" Mom asks Peter and Michael.

They look from Mom to Dad, Dad to Mom and burst into tears. They did not want to make such a choice. Dad, not wanting them to have to make such a choice either, turns around and leaves the Luchenza

Station with sadness dragging his shoulders down and my sadness settles in my heart, sadness for Dad and for Geraldine and for my brothers' crying, and for me. "Get in the car boys. You're coming to Warren's house." Mom tells them.

Warren's house, where Mom has chickens again. Warrens house, where Michael, after returning from playing with friends one afternoon, opens the bedroom door to find Dad in bed with Mom, on Mom, in Warren's bed. He told me Mom looked over Dad's shoulder, and said, "Is that you, Michael?"

"Ye-ye-yes." Michael has always stuttered, ever since he was almost electrocuted. He nearly died – in fact he would have died if Peter hadn't been on the roof too and pulled him off the live wire he had grabbed with both his hands. He was badly burnt from his hands to the soles of his feet. Mom says that's why he stutters.

"Go and feed the chickens," Mom said.

"O-o-k-k-kay," He answered, reversing out the door, confused.

Yes, there was much confusion in Warren's confusing house.

Mom and Warren always fought when they drank, usually ending with Mom screaming and running to hide in bushes at night, with me, always me, scrambling after her, to hide with her, to dab at her bleeding nose or bleeding lip or bleeding eyebrow.

And then there was the fight one day in the bar at the Limbe Country Club that everyone was talking about, Peter said. Mom had left her bar stool to visit the loo. On her return she swung her handbag at the back of Warren's unsuspecting head, nearly knocking him off his bar stool.

"BASTARD."

WHACK.

Was it something he'd said?

Was it something he'd done, that she had stewed over in the bathroom? Whatever it was, she whacked him again, and took off screaming. Out of the bar, past club members gathered at tables on the verandah, sipping their gin and tonics. Heads turn left. Heads turn right. Eyes follow Mom as she disappears around the side of the club.

Now comes red faced, bug eyed, Warren. "Get back here, you bitch." He also passes those silent swivel-heads, heads that follow him left, then right. Just like watching a tennis match.

Catching sight of a ladder that workmen had left leaning against the eaves of the roof, Mom, hand over hand, scrambled up the rungs. Up she went. Up, up and onto the clubhouse roof. Perched above the gin and tonic drinkers.

Warren, spotting the ladder, grins, pauses at the bottom of the ladder for a second before he yanks it away from the wall, shoves it over and down onto the lawn. Flop. Plop. He returns to the bar, a smile on his face. Heads turn left. Tongues wag.

"It's awful, the way they carry on."

"Isn't it just? It's dreadful."

Much later. "She's been on the roof a long time."

"I know. It's very quiet up there. Do you think she has fallen asleep?"

"Can someone please help me?" Mom pleads, as though she had heard the chatter and remembered where she was. She doesn't want to be up there anymore. Nobody answers her plea.

"BENSON, BRING THE LADDER," Mom yells. Benson, the black barman, knows there is nothing he can do about this situation.

Club members on the verandah below sip their G & T's, exchange looks, raise their eyebrows, shrug their shoulders. There is the odd tsk-tsk. But no one makes a move. They dare not incur the wrath of Warren.

Golfers straggle back from a Saturday-afternoon game, glance idly up at Mom,

"What on earth is Pamela doing up there on the roof?" they seem to say shaking their heads, shrug, continue their way to the Dog Box. The Dog Box is the "men only" watering hole on the 18th hole of the golf course. There, cold beers are the order of the day.

Mom would like to be in the Dog Box. She is really, but it's not the dog box she wants to be in. She'd like to be perched on a bar stool at the 18th hole Dog Box with all the men in her sights and a whiskey in her hand. Instead she is on this bloody uncomfortable roof being ignored by everyone and getting more sober by the minute.

"Bwana Cluff, the Dona has been up there a long time. Perhaps I can be putting the ladder back now," Benson ventures.

"E-bloody-Ikona, Benson, she stays up there until I'm ready to let her down, *if* I let her down." Warren nursing his fourth or fifth whiskey since Mom had whacked him over the head with her handbag is showing signs of his over-indulgence. Finally, he staggers out to the parking lot and his Morris Minor and wends his way out of the club grounds. God help the cyclists.

As soon as Benson is sure the coast is clear, he runs outside and replaces the ladder. "Dona Fitzgerald, you can come down now, the Bwana, he has gone," he says.

Mom, quite sober by now, sheepishly descends and returns to the bar, eyes left. Back in the bar perched on a barstool she powders her nose and refreshes her lipstick, then runs a brush through her hair.

Benson, a witness to much of this sort of carrying-on, commiserates with her while pouring her a whiskey on the rocks. "Dona, you must not be hitting the Bwana with your handbag, he has a very bad temper."

"I know, Benson, I know."

She knows but that doesn't stop her.

Not then, not ever.

MALARIA, MORE MAYHEM AND THE LONGDROP

The rhythmic beating of drums gets loud, louder, even louder. Close, closer, closer to my bedroom. The noise gets into my head. It bangs against my skull.

CRASH. BANG. CRASH. The bedroom wall collapses.

Fierce warriors with leopard skin loincloths leap over the tumbled bricks, whooping and hollering, shaking spears at me. Their eyes white translucent marbles set in sweaty, shiny, black faces.

Stop. Stop. Stop. My hands hold and squeeze my head. My mouth is wide open, screaming. No. No.

"Rosebud, Rosebud what's the matter?" Mom, running into my room, asks.

What's the matter! Can't she see what the matter is? Can't she see them? Can't she see there is just a big hole where my wall used to be?

Can't she hear them?

No. No she cannot. Only I can.

It's another bout of malaria.

Along with malaria come nightmares and cravings. This time around, I crave Lemon & Barley squash with ice. Peter, who also has malaria, craves Lemon & Barley too.

Answering our cravings was Billie Thorne, who drove all the way out to the house to bring us Robinson's Lemon & Barley with ice. Billie Thorne is married to Mom's solicitor, Leonard Thorne. Mom and Dad are finally going ahead with a divorce and have custody battles going on about us. Billie is a bad alcoholic. "Poor thing," Mom always said, "She was in a Japanese concentration camp during the war. The Japanese used to stick needles under her finger nails."

"Poppycock!" Leonard would say, "Billie was never in a Japanese camp." It makes a good story though, and Mom, who liked good stories, is not going to let this one go.

Even though Billie is drunk a lot, I like her. She always makes mom laugh. Today, she makes me laugh, before she makes me feel sick. She and Mom sit by my bed and Billie recites a funny rhyme she knows I like. She wrote it out for me so that I could recite it along with her, but I cannot do it with her accent:

One day as I sat in my
umba-jumba chamber,

I saw a raticum-paticum eating
my haticum-paticum paynee.

If I hadna' my stick, ma stole,
ma stick, ma staynee,

I'd a' beaten that raticum-
paticum paynee.

Billie cries a lot. She doesn't cry now, not today, as she leans over me to feel my forehead. My stomach churns when I look down the gaping front of her dress. I see stringy breasts, empty sack breasts, with long black hairs around the nipples and I can smell the whiskey on her breath. Billie always has whiskey-breath, only today she's not drunk, not really drunk. She is tending the sick, you see. Really drunk will come later.

When she leaves she gives a dismissive wave of her hand and a toss of her head as she goes out the door. "With tha' she swep' out," she says over her shoulder in her Cockney accent.

What comes next into my befuddled mind is Michael. He stands by my bed, telling me a stupid story about the chameleon he found. This chameleon he says is now living on a branch in his bedroom.

"Michael you have told me that about ten times! I'm sick of hearing it. Sick of it."

"Mom, Rosebud is delirious again, I told her about my chameleon and she says I have told her ten times, I haven't, Mom. It's the first time I've told her. I only just got my chameleon."

Rubbish. I've heard about that chameleon many times. I have. I know I have.

"Michael, that's what malaria does to you. Rosebud believes she has heard it before."

In another day or two I am a bit better. The fever, the hot-and-cold shivers, the nightmares are gone. But I am still in bed because I'm weak. Peter and Michael bring me Bovril toast.

"Here, Rosebud, we made you some Bovril toast."

"Thank you, thank you."

I'm surprised they did this for me. How nice. They know I love Bovril toast. I take a bite as they scurry from my bedroom, giggling. Why? Why are those brothers of mine giggling, I wonder as I bite down on the toast.

This is disgusting! The Bovril sticks to the roof of my mouth, my teeth. Spit. Spit. Spit. YUCK. What is this? It's black like Bovril but it's not Bovril.

"Mom, Mom, come here! Come here! What is this? It's not Bovril. What is it Mom?"

It was tick blood! My brothers had burst a fat, grey tick, spreading its blood on my toast. When Mom found out, she nearly burst. "Jesus wept and mother cried! You little buggers, don't you know you could make your sister sick, very, very sick? Just when she is getting over malaria."

I didn't get sick from that tick blood, though I came down with malaria again. Doctor Antou has told Mom I will have to leave Nyasaland. If I get another bout of malaria, it could turn into blackwater fever. By then, I'd had malaria about five times –so much in fact that I am yellow again, yellow as the day I was born.

No steps to eradicate the malaria mosquito had been taken in Nyasaland, not in those days. To prevent it, I was supposed to take a quinine tablet every day. I'd forget and so would Mom.

Following Doctor Antou's advice, I am sent off to Aunt Patty and her husband Uncle Ernie in Rhodesia. I arrive in Bulawayo with yellow skin and yellow eyes. There would be no malaria here but there would be mayhem. Oh yes, there would be plenty of that.

Aunt Patty and Uncle Ernie and their daughters Irene and Muriel, and their sons Reggie and Ernest live on a farm in Khami, which is about 10 miles from the city of Bulawayo. It's not really a farm since there is no farming actually done on their land. There is only one cow and Nyama a young Shona farm hand to milk it. Nothing else that could possibly earn the name "farm." Nevertheless, it's called a farm, deserving or not.

Here I would be for the next three years, sometimes flying back to Nyasaland for the school holidays and coming back with new clothes. I felt bad about the clothes because Irene did not have many clothes. I would share them with her. I loved my cousins. Reggie, two years younger than me, Ernest and Muriel younger still, and Irene one year older than me. I adored Aunty Patty. Uncle Ernie? Well, he was always nice to me. It was just that when he drank that he was meaner than a snake to everyone else.

Mom had sent money for my brown pleated tunic Evelyn School uniform, white blouse and brown shoes, one of them built-up to stop the twisting. It would be the first and last pair of un-twisting shoes I would own, which was fine with me. I hated those ugly shoes. I think everyone forgot about the build-up and I was not going to remind anyone. Besides, most of the time I was barefoot like my cousins.

This house I will now live in is half-built. It sits in its ramshackle state on ten acres of bush, boulders and huge anthills. There is a small dam with a slimy bottom you never want your feet to touch. The house had remained half-built for many years. I don't know why. Perhaps no one has enough money to finish it.

There is a bedroom for Aunt Patty and Uncle Ernie and a bedroom for all five of us kids. It has four twin beds. Muriel and Ernest slept top to tail. An unfinished bathroom between these two bedrooms has a galvanized iron tub. Water for baths has to be heated on an outside woodstove.

The kitchen-cum-dining-cum-everything room is sparsely furnished with a fridge, a stove and a table against the wall with four straight-backed kitchen chairs. Uncle Ernie would sit on his chair at the head of the table, one foot on the ground, the other on the chair with his leg drawn up and his knee under his chin, wheezing from a hole in his back. That hole, he told us, was from a war wound. Aunty Patty says it was from pneumonia and something to do with his lung. He'd usually have a tankard of beer or a glass of whiskey in one hand and a cold Lucky Strike in the other. He keeps his Lucky Strikes in the fridge, so they stay fresh, he says.

There is a hallway that runs from the kitchen, past the bedrooms to what was meant to be the front door. There is no door, just the opening for a door and then a drop of about three feet to the dirt. It is not used to enter or exit. It is used as a lookout for comings and goings on the long, dusty driveway, especially to see if Aunty Patty is making her weary way home from Lobel's Bakery in Bulawayo, where she does the books for Mr. Lobel.

To the one side of the hallway, opposite Aunty Pat and Uncle Ernie's bedroom is another door-less room, intended as a future lounge. No such grand room was in its future that I could see. It's a large ugly oblong room with a dirt floor and rusted, pane-less windows. There is no ceiling, just an asbestos corrugated roof. We call it the Long Room. It is used for hanging dripping muslin bags of sour milk and spiced strips of raw meat. They dangle from hooks on wires strung high up waiting to dry out, to become cottage cheese and biltong. It's also the room where Aunt Patty once put large jars of pineapple beer to ferment, then forgot about them until they exploded one night, one after the other, like gun shots, send-ing us all under our beds in terror. We thought Uncle Ernie was on a rampage with his shotgun again.

Irene and I painted life-sized pin-ups in bikinis on the walls of this long room. We think them stun-ning works of art. Aunt Patty thinks they cheer up the dismal place. Uncle Ernie? He just grunts.

This whole ugly house is covered with a corru-gated roof, some of it iron, some of it asbestos, held down with boulders.

When it rains, we have to run for pots and basins to catch the drops of water that leak through the rusted holes here and there. The pitter-patter of the rain and the drip, drip, drip in the pots and basins is a lovely sound to me. It is still my safe sound.

Then there is the other place. The horrible place, three hundred feet from the house. The *outhouse.*

It's not an easy walk to the outhouse, not because of the distance, though it was far if you needed to go badly, but because it was so primitive. That's what made it a difficult walk.

I hate that I have to go to the bathroom in this door-less shack that exposes me to anyone else who wants to use the hole in the ground, this pit we call the Longdrop. Rusty nails pop out its rotten wooden walls and huge spiders hang in webs from the rusted, holey corrugated iron roof. Scorpions scuttle around the dirt floor.

If I listen carefully I may be able to hear the crunch of gravel when someone is coming. Then I can shout: "I'm in here!" I don't like to do that because I hate anyone knowing that I poop and pee. I know they know I do, but I cling to the notion that they may think I am above such things. Just as I cling to the sides of this wooden seat, with my arms stiff, so as to keep my bum in the air and my cheeks above that seat. I don't want my bottom to hang in the hole with all those writhing, glistening maggots four feet below.

I can hardly bear the thought of the maggots and I certainly can't bear the awful smell. I want to pinch my nose with my fingers, but I dare not let go of the seat. So, I wrinkle my nose, close my mouth and hold my breath. Hold my breath until I think I am going to faint.

When I'm done, I have a bigger problem. How do I reach the torn squares of newspaper looped onto a piece of string to wipe myself? I am not strong enough to hold myself up, like gymnasts do, with one arm. The only thing I can do is rest my left bum cheek onto the very edge of the seat. I squeeze my eyes shut and snatch the paper with my right hand and my right bum cheek falls to the seat. For a split second I sit in alarm, shudder, then bounce up off that seat, forgetting about the scorpions, as though I had sat on a hornet's nest. I wipe my bum with the black ink of old news, then reach for my pants which are sitting on my knees because I didn't want them to touch the floor. Now they're on the floor around my feet where they fell when I bounced up. I pull them up my shuddering legs and let my skirt fall from my lap where I had screwed it up in a ball, and skedaddle out of there as fast as I can.

I'm as anxious leaving this place as I am going to it because I know I'm going to have to come back, sooner or later. I try not to think of the fact that there will have to be other visits, hopefully not at night. If it's just a number one I can use the potty under the bed but if it's a number two I have to make the walk in the dark with a torch. There is a hook to hang the torch on, but its light does not reach the dark corners, where snakes could slither into between the time I checked the corner and hung up the torch.

It is at times like these that I wish I could go home to mom and an indoor toilet smelling of pine. I will be so happy when I can sit on a toilet seat again and pull a chain.

Uncle Ernie spends a lot of time in the horrible place. He doesn't seem to mind it. When Aunt Patty would ask: "Where's your father?" The answer would usually be in unison: "Longdrop."

He would sit in the Longdrop on his haunches for hours, or so it seemed, with a newspaper or book. The explosions coming from that place when he was there earned him a secret whispered name… Rumble Bum.

"It's a dreadful state of affairs that Patty has to live in that house, that hovel, like a poor white," Mom would say, conveniently setting aside the fact that eight years earlier she was momentarily prepared to accept such living conditions for herself. Back then, eight years ago, she had brought Peter, Michael and me from Filabusi, where Dad remained, to look after

Irene, while Aunt Patty gave birth to Reggie. Years later, Aunt Patty had said she should have been suspicious: Mom brings three children to look after one. On Aunt Patty's return from the hospital with her ten-day old son, Mom and Uncle Ernie stood in the doorway to her bedroom and announced that they were in love with each other.

"You have a son now, Patty. He can look after you in your old age," Uncle Ernie said.

"Sorry Patty, it just happened," Mom said.

Aunt Patty contacted Dad and he said, "Come to me, Patty. Let them have each other."

"You can have each other," she tells them, "I'm going to Gerry."

That was not what Mom wanted to hear. She goes back to Dad. She had proved she could have her sister's husband and now she didn't want him anymore. She was lucky that Aunt Patty probably loved her more than she loved Uncle Ernie. Otherwise she may have had all her hair cut off. That is what Aunt Patty did to a woman Uncle Ernie was having an affair with just after Irene was born. She hid around the corner from Uncle Ernie's electrical shop with a pair of scissors and when the woman came out, she grabbed her by the hair and cut big chunks out of it. All the while the woman was screaming, and Uncle Ernie was trying to pull Aunt Patty off her.

Then there is the body-shuddering memory in a bubble. A memory of screams and thud, thud, thud, in the middle of the night, coming from Aunt Patty and Uncle Ernie's room, where mom was sleeping. I don't know where Aunt Patty and Uncle Ernie were, but I hear a woman's voice a voice I don't recognize.

"Beat her, Larry, beat her, beat her. Teach the bitch a lesson." Thud, crash. "Sleep with my husband again and I will kill you, you bitch," the female voice yells.

Then there were the pictures, pictures for the solicitor. Pictures of Mom with black eyes swollen shut, matted bloody hair, puffed up mouth, black and blue bruises on her face, arms, chest, stomach. Pictures imprinted on my young mind in vivid technicolour.

Years later, I learnt that mom had been at a party where Peggy, a cousin of mom's, was at the same party with her husband Larry Louth. Mom had gone outside with Larry and they had sex in the bushes. Larry Louth, the lout, told his wife that Mom had seduced him. Peggy said if Larry didn't beat Pamela up she would file for a divorce. That is what had brought them out to the farm in the early hours of the morning.

Larry and Peggy Louth remained names that sent cold shivers through my body and left a sick feeling in my stomach, dangerous names that made me want to run and hide.

Sleep with my husband again and I will kill you, words that confuse and terrify me.

Why would Mom sleep with Larry? Where were Aunt Patty and Uncle Ernie that night? Why couldn't someone save Mom from such a brutal beating? Dad wasn't there. He must have been in Filabusi. So many unanswered questions, so many shadowy, sinister people in that bubble.

I think a lot of love that Aunt Patty had had for Uncle Ernie once transferred to her animals. She always had Rhodesian ridgebacks. She also had a bulldog called Churchill. She adored Churchill and when he did not meet her after work one Saturday. we went in search of him. We found him on the ground behind the house. He was barely alive. Blood oozed out of his ears and mouth. Nyama had said he thought one of the natives from the compound had given him ground glass mixed into raw meat.

"Why? Why? Why?" Aunt Patty wailed, all the while cradling her beloved Churchill, kissing and kissing him, rocking him back and forth in her arms. "Why would someone do that, Nyama?"

"They're frightened of him, Missus."

Churchill dies, and Aunt Patty mourns for weeks. She says if she could find the bastard that did this cruel thing she would kill him with her bare hands.

> *If I hadna' my stick, ma stole,*
> *ma stick, ma staynees,*
>
> *I'd have beaten that raticum-*
> *paticum paynee.*

Why would anyone be frightened of Churchill unless they are up to no good? That's my new worry.

I'm afraid of almost everything. I never stand next to my bed. I leap on it from a distance, as I'm sure there is someone, or something, under there ready to grab me by the ankles. And now there is a poisoner lurking around. I am an-almost-twelve-year-old-scaredy-cat, only feeling safe when it rains.

SNOW BALL, A MAN'S THING AND NYAMA'S NEW KAIA

She is pure white, this baby kitten I'd been given as something to love because I have lost my family. Avril is with Mom, Geraldine is in boarding school in Blantyre, Peter and Michael are in boarding school in Salisbury and I'm here in Bulawayo living with Aunt Patty and Uncle Ernie because of the malaria. I cried so much when Mom wrote to tell me her and Dad's divorce was final. I suppose I was hoping for a miracle. Aunt Patty gave me this kitten. A white, ball of fluff with pink-rimmed eyes and a pink nose. I name her Snow Ball and I take her to bed with me, where she purrs and snuggles and cuddles into my neck.

In the morning Snow Ball is dead. Aunt Patty finds me sitting up in my bed, sobbing, tears falling down my cheeks and dripping onto Snow Ball's limp little body. "I killed her, Aunt Patty. I killed her."

"Oh, Rosebud darling, it was an accident. An accident. She may not have lived anyway. She was a sickly little thing."

No, she was not. She was murdered, murdered by me. I trapped her under my big body. I can't bear the thought that she must have been struggling to breathe. A killer, that's what I am.

I bury Snow Ball's soft tiny body in my old pajama top, and spend hours beside her grave every chance I get, telling her how sorry I am for killing her. "I didn't mean to," I tell her. "I loved you."

No one can console me. I feel her squashed little body on my back, where she remained for a long, long time.

Slowly, I push that defenseless little kitten to a special place in my heart, because school has started, and I must mind my P's and Q's at this new school. I can't be crying about my kitten all the time, can I?

Most mornings Uncle Ernie would drop us at school and we'd get the bus back to the house. It was a long, dusty walk from the bus stop and on scorching days the two miles seem like ten. The only thing to be done was to just do it, perspiring and lugging your satchel. Sometimes kicking stones or stopping to inspect a beetle or some other insect. "Don't dawdle, and keep your hats on," Aunt Patty would tell Irene, Reggie and me.

Well, no one could have told me about the 12-year-old Afrikaans boy who lived on a farm close to ours. His name is Johannes. One day he runs up to me just as Irene and I get to the top of our long drive, shoves a piece of rumpled paper into my hand, runs away.

Written in pencil on that scrunched-up piece of paper: *I will give you 2/6 (two shillings and sixpence) if you let me fuck you.*

My face gets hot, as I stare at those words.

"What is it?" Irene asks, "Let me see that, let me see it."

I hand it to her.

"What a cheek! You have to show this to Mom. You have to, Rosebud"

And so, I do. "Look what that Afrikaans boy next door gave me today, Aunt Patty."

Aunt Patty is so angry she takes the letter next door to show the boy's father. Johannes's father makes him carry a big rock while running around the wall of their dam, whipping him every time his arms sag. Beating his back, his legs.

Johannes's hoarse cries and pleading hurts my chest. I jam my fingers into my ears. Still, I hear him.

Why did I show Aunt Patty the letter? Why? Why did she have to take it to his father?

I feel much worse about his beating than I do about the letter. I never see him again.

Sometimes Rumble Bum picks us up from school if he left his shop early. He owns the shop: Rice Electrical, so he can leave whenever he wants to. When this happened, it meant we didn't have that long walk home. It also meant that often he would stop at the men-only bar in the Standard Hotel. Then we would have to sit in the hot car for ages, maybe as long as two hours, sometimes even longer.

Rumble Bum had picked us up this hot day in October. October, suicide month it's called because it gets so hot people commit suicide, or so they say.

"Reggie, please go and ask Dad for a Coke."

"Ach man Irene, you know he won't buy us Cokes."

"Please, Reggie, try. Maybe he's in a good mood today."

Reggie is back in a minute and he's not holding any Cokes.

"I told you he wouldn't. He said no, we're going home soon."

"He is so mean."

We don't know the man that comes to the open window on my side of the car, unzips his fly, takes his thingy out and shakes it at my face. I roll up the window with shaking hands and he laughs, showing me all his rotten brown-tobacco-stained teeth. The two front teeth are missing and his lizard tongue darts in and out of the gap.

"Go away," Irene shouts, "Go away or I will call my Dad."

He leaves, still shaking his thing and laughing.

Ach sis man!

SIS! We all shout and laugh, now that he has gone.

Wait until we tell Aunt Patty about this, she is going to be so cross!

Rumble Bum is drunk when he comes out of the bar, really drunk. So drunk he drives home on the wrong side of the road. Cars swerve, hoot their hooters. Drivers shake their fists at us.

Irene shouts at Rumble Bum all the way home. When Uncle Ernie gets out of the car at the farm, there is a really big wet patch on his khaki shorts. With a bottle of whiskey in one hand and a quart of Castle Lager in the other, he stumbles into the house.

He drinks the beer then he goes to his room to sleep for a few hours before he starts on the whiskey.

Now we had all better watch out.

All of us kids wait for Aunt Patty at the bottom of the drive, as we do every day. She is always tired from her long walk from the bus stop. At five thirty she appears through the shimmering heat and we immediately bombard her with all the day's happenings, sparing her none of it for her weariness.

"We had to wait in the car outside the bar for two hours today."

"He wouldn't even buy us a Coke. It was so hot."

"He drove home on the wrong side of the road"

"Yes, and cars were hooting at us."

"A man put his thingy up to Rosebud's window and shook it."

"Dad wet himself in the car. He had a big wet patch on his pants."

"I hate him, Mom, he is a drunkard, I want him to die, Mom," Irene said.

"Irene, don't talk like that. He's still your father."

"I don't care. Please tell him not to pick us up from school again. It was very, very scary in the car. I thought we were going to crash."

"Ernie," Aunt Patty says as she walks into the kitchen, "I don't want you picking up the kids from school anymore."

"Who do you think you are? Huh?" He lunges at her, "Don't you dare tell me what I can or can't do with my own kids," With that he punches her in the face. Mayhem, like the blood from Aunt Patty's nose, erupts. Kids screaming and Irene swearing at her father. "COWARD," she yells, "You bloody coward." Tugging pulling Aunt Patty, we get her into our room and barricade the door.

This is how it always ends when Uncle Ernie drinks.

The next day Aunt Patty, with a black eye and swollen red nose, pleads, "Irene, please don't antagonize your father while I'm at work. Please just keep out of his way."

Irene does keep out of his way for a few days. It doesn't last though. Soon she is back to giving him cheek. She couldn't keep her mouth shut when he picked on her. One afternoon she goes too far with her backtalk. Uncle Ernie chases her out of the house, his shotgun in his hands. She flees out the door-less-door, down the drive.

BOOM. Uncle Ernie fires a shot over her head, "If you come back to this house I will kill you. I will!"

He means it. We know he does, so we send Reggie to call the police from the call box at the bus stop.

Rumble Bum is a charmer, but he couldn't charm the policeman that came that day, the policeman who listens to his lies, then takes us outside, one by one. "What happened here this afternoon?" he asks, and we tell him.

Back in the kitchen the policeman says, "Mister Rice, I believe these children. Out of the mouths of babes, they say. I should arrest you, sir, but I'm going to give you the benefit of the doubt. I want you to know, though, that I will arrest you if anything like this ever happens again and then you will go to jail, Mister Rice."

Ooooo YES, please take him to jail. We want him to go to jail, NOW. NOW. Not next time.

We keep away from Uncle Ernie when Aunt Patty is at work and look for things to do that will keep us outside.

The farm's terrain is very rocky. Flat rocks, round rocks, rocks balancing on rocks. There is one special rock I would sometimes go to when I wanted to be on my own. It was a large, flat rock with a hollowed basin which, when I lay on it, cradled my body perfectly. I loved to lie on this rock and bask in the sun, lizard-like. The warm rays seeping into my pores was a delicious feeling.

One afternoon as I lay relishing the warmth, dreaming silly dreams of knights in shining armour whisking me away while the cooing of doves lull me. Out of the corner of my eye I see it, a scorpion. It's huge pincers agape, and its vertebrate tail curved upward in the shape of a cee, ready to strike. My chest tightens; I know I am in danger. The scorpion and I are dead still. Eyeing each other, time stops, the cooing of doves, hushed. Then a calm acceptance descends my body, a strange sort of fatalism. The scorpion turns suddenly and scuttles under a rock. Just like that the danger passes and allows me to jump up and scuttle off too, away from the rock that felt so safe a few seconds ago and I know that scorpion has robbed me of this warm place, forever.

I never go back to that rock. Instead Irene and I take our books down to the dam where we sit on the edge and dangle our feet in the water while reading our books. My favourite book, aside from a biography about Anna Pavlova, is *A Woman Called Fancy* by Frank Yerby. I want to be Fancy and Anna Pavlova.

Irene reads what Aunt Patty calls "Penny Horribles," short romance novels, each one like the last with names changed.

One day, going to the dam I very nearly stand on a puff adder. It's a fat snake, as puff adders are and it's curled up, basking in the sun. My foot misses it by inches! They are sluggish snakes and usually only bite if you step on them. So Reggie says. He knows a lot about snakes. I'm careful where I put my feet after that.

We also come across a dead chameleon with its mouth open and its tongue burnt out. Nyama tells us that a lot of natives think the chameleon is evil because it's one eye looks forward while the other one looks back. They burn the end of a stick in the fire and then push the ember into the chameleon's mouth.

This makes me very sad. Why are there so many cruel things? My mind goes over and over these things and I know I will think about that helpless chameleon, just as I think about Snow Ball, with an ache in my chest.

"Tomorrow, let's fix up the old hut next to Nyama's kaia," Irene suggests.

"Okay, let's."

We start by throwing huge dollops of mud at the walls that have holes in them where the old mud had fallen off.

Nyama milks the cow and sweeps the dirt yard, sprinkling it with water to keep the dust down. He has a hut on the property, in a clearing ringed by trees, quite far away from the house. Nyama means meat – flesh in Fanagalo. Why anyone would call a child meat I don't know. We all love Nyama. He is such a kind man. He is our friend. And right now, he is very amused at our mud throwing, shaking his head and clicking his tongue.

"Just you wait and see Nyama, it's going to be a mush kaia," Irene says, as we slather the mud, inside and out, smoothing it with wet rags. When the mud dries, we smooth layer upon layer of cow dung on the inside. The dung must also dry out between layers, so this takes weeks. As the hut takes shape Nyama begins to take us seriously. We have his attention now. Bit-by-bit he joins us in this building of a hut. He puts a thatched roof on and we start the floor.

More layers of dung. Smooth. Dung, smooth. When it's very dry we wax it with black stoop polish, wax, shine, wax, shine, until the floor looks like glass and we look like black piccanins.

However, there is a major thing missing on this hut.

A door.

The unused front door to the house has been leaning against the carport for years. Nobody sees it anymore. We sneak it up to the hut. Rumble Bum won't notice, we know he won't, and even if he does we shall deny all knowledge of its disappearance.

"Door? What door?" we will say.

"Ikona, ikona," (No, no,) Nyama says, "The baas he will be too angry. Take it back. Take it back."

"Ikona, Nyama, it's your door now, we are giving it to you, but don't say anything to anyone, okay?"

Nyama is still worried about the darn door but we refuse to take it back. We make him cut it down to fit.

It's a palace, this hut.

"One day I am going to build myself a hut," I declare.

"Me, too." Irene agrees.

"Me, too." Reggie echoes.

Nyama loves his new kaia and we celebrate by eating caterpillars and flying ants with him. He squeezes the yellow insides out of the caterpillars and fries the skins along with the headless flying ants. It will rain tomorrow because there are a zillion flying ants all about. We get the ones that have dropped their wings. Flying ants taste like peanut butter. We eat these delicacies with sticky sudza, cooked mealie meal, rolled into balls between our palms, sitting on our haunches, like Nyama, around the fire. Admiring our handy-work,

"Now maybe you will get yourself a wife, Nyama, now that you have such a nice kaia for her," I say.

He laughs, showing us his pink gums and a mouthful of teeth as white as Snow Ball's fur.

GREAT-AUNT POLLY GOES UP IN A PUFF OF SMOKE

Hundreds and hundreds of twirling, dancing, twisting, white feathers greet us when we break the door down. Some hover in the thick air, quivering, waiting for their turn to dance in this smoke-filled room where a mattress on an iron bed frame smolders and smokes.

The bed is Great Aunt Polly's, mom and Aunt Patty's aunt who lives close to us in Bulawayo. She's half under it. Dead.

We knew one day Great Aunt Polly would go up in a puff of smoke. We just didn't know about the feathers.

The skin on half of Aunt Polly's body, the part under the bed, glows a bright pink. Large glassy blisters sit, here and there, as though the pores of her skin had blown bubbles. Her hennaed hair, an orange frizz, frizzled up on one side.

The skin on the other half, the half not under the bed, looks quite normal except for the curved feathers, gently rocking, back and forth, back and forth, on her body, on the floor and on her bedside table, where the empty gin bottle sits.

We stare, Aunt Patty, Irene, Reggie and me, stare at these feathers that lift lazily into the air every time someone opens the door, lift to briefly twist and twirl, before slowly sinking back to Aunt Polly, to the floor, as though they were tired of this dance now.

The smoke and feathers have enshrouded the room with silence, an eerie hush.

My head tingles and all I hear in that otherwise quiet room, is a ringing in my ears.

She must have pulled the burning pillows out from under her head, we surmise, releasing all those feathers from their cotton case like escaped prisoners not knowing where to go.

Did she then roll off the bed and pull herself half under it? We think so.

That's how we found her on that Sunday, dear-sweet-ugly-great-aunt Polly. Aunt Polly was my grandmother's youngest, plain sister. She and her Gordon's Gin had not arrived for their usual Saturday night sleepover. Aunt Patty sent Nyama to check on her in her little one-room house on a large, isolated plot a couple of miles from us, for it was unusual that she had not come.

He'd returned, Nyama had, with his eyes popping out of his head, his body trembling. "Tshetsha, tshetsha, figa maningi ntutu. Tumuch ntutu pagati the madam's kaia. (Quickly, quickly, come lots of smoke. Too much smoke inside the madam's house).

Yes, there was too much smoke in her house and too many feathers and too much sadness.

There will be no more singing, at least not by Great Aunt Polly, of: "*You take the high road and I'll take the low road and I'll be in Scotland afore ye.*" She would, most often, pass out with that song on her lips, that song about her beloved Scotland, with a burning cigarette between her fingers. One of us would gently remove the cigarette so as not to wake her.

There would be no ballet lessons for me now, either. She was going to send Irene to elocution lessons and me to ballet, because everyone, including me, especially me, believed I would be a ballerina one day. Famous I'd be, like Anna Pavlova, like Moira Shearer in "Red Shoes."

When Mom visited from Nyasaland, I'd put on a show for Aunt Patty, Aunt Polly and Mom. My cousins as well, dancing on tip toes. Wildly I ran, here, there, here, twirling as ballerinas do, before dying at the feet of this adoring, awed audience, my hands crossed at the wrists, my swan's head on the floor between my winged arms.

"She is going to make our fortune one day, Patty," Mom said.

"Of course, she will, Pammy, I know that." Aunt Patty replied.

"She must go to Ballet School," Great Aunt Polly piped up.

All that has gone now.

Gone in a puff of smoke and feathers, just like that, POOF!

Later, on that same Sunday we'd found Aunt Polly burnt to death, Uncle Ernie shot a baby. First, we heard the shot, then the baby crying. Bulging-eyed once again, we bolt into the back yard. Did he shoot a piccanin?

Lying on the ground is the most beautiful creature I'd ever seen. It is a baby deer, crying, just like a human baby, tears tumbling out of its big gorgeous green eyes. "How could you shoot a baby deer? How could you? I hate you. I hate you," I scream at Uncle Ernie.

"I hate you. I hate you. You coward," Irene cries.

"Get back in the house." Uncle Ernie growls at us, "Now."

We go back, our shoulders heaving, our heads down, our fingers in our ears, trying to block out the sound of the crying. But even with our fingers in our ears we hear the second shot.

The crying stops.

She is dead. At least we think it's a she.

In our beds that night, we cry. Cry, for Great Aunt Polly. Cry for the baby deer. "How can anyone shoot a baby deer? It still had its spots." Irene asks.

"How can anyone shoot any deer?" I sob.

"Rosebud, will we ever see Aunt Polly again?" Muriel asks.

"No, we won't, Muriel, she has gone to heaven."

"I hope they don't let her smoke there, in heaven," says Muriel.

In my prayers I ask God to please let Uncle Ernie fall in the Longdrop.

I write to Mom about the deer. I tell her how much I hate Uncle Ernie. He's a maggot, I say; he should be at the bottom of the Longdrop with the other maggots.

The next morning Aunt Patty gives us each a six-pence so that we can buy a doughnut from the stand at school. These round doughnuts, bigger than tennis balls, are the very best doughnuts in the world. What they are is yeasty bread dough with apricot jam in the middle and large sugar crystals on the outside. They're a special treat for all of us.

This treat on this day is because we all had to go to school with puffy eyes. Aunt Patty's eyes are all poofed with puffiness too. Rumble Bum? He just sits on his chair, puffing on his Lucky Strike. All puffed up, he is, the big, brave white hunter. He'd cut up that baby deer and strips of its spiced flesh hang from hooks in the Longroom, drying. Soon it will be biltong (dried meat), biltong I vow I will never, ever, eat. I can't even look up at those strips. All I can see are the big tears rolling down that baby's face, her big, sad eyes asking, why? I want to ask too, *why*. Why Aunt Polly, why this baby deer?

Why couldn't Uncle Ernie have been the one to go in a puff of smoke and feathers?

I will be flying back to Nyasaland for the school holidays in a few days and I can hardly wait to get away from this place of death.

PAMELA'S HAIRDRESSING SALON AND THE CAT THAT CREPT

I take the sadness with me on that big old Dakota aeroplane that makes me airsick. I am almost fourteen, old enough to fly on my own now Mom had said. Air- hostesses bring me paper bags to vomit in. "Keep your head up," they tell me. Is it the sadness I am vomiting up? All the sadness of Aunt Polly, Snow Ball, the baby deer, the chameleon, the fighting, the going of Dad. Can sadness make you sick?

The lady next to me demands to be moved to a vacant seat somewhere else on the plane.

When the Dakota makes it's bone-rattling landing at Chileka Airport in Blantyre, all us passengers must remain seated while personnel walk through the cabin spraying DDT from a flit pump, just in case we have brought the Tsetse fly in with us. They pump and flit over our heads, flit under our seats, flit, flit down the aisle, flit, and flit on the ceiling. When the flitting stops, we are allowed to disembark. Which we do, and we greet those who have come to collect us, reeking of DDT.

With wobbly legs I kiss Mom, look down as I greet Warren. I had hoped he'd be gone, hoped he was out of Mom's life by now.

"Rosebud, you look so pale. Are you alright?"

"I was sick the whole trip, Mom. I hate that plane."

During those six weeks, I would spend most of my time helping Mom in her hairdressing salon, washing customers' hair, passing Mom curlers, making tea. I also spend a lot of time just hanging out at the window, scouting to see who is coming and going on that street below. I would report all these happenings to Mom: "Mrs. Trataris is going into the tailor. She has a new car. It's a red convertible."

The Trataris's own a large bakery, supplying most of the bread in Nyasaland. Mr. Trataris is Greek, and Mrs. Trataris is black. This in itself was scandalous. He'd gone native. Fraternizing was bad enough but marrying a black! Really! The Trataris's would now become the subject of much discussion between Mom and her ladies.

"Do you think he made his money from baking bread, Pamela?"

"Not likely, my dear."

"They do spoil that son of theirs, George. He's a real playboy."

"Their daughter, Helen, is a lovely girl. She plays the piano beautifully you know."

This is how it goes, until I report on a new curiosity out there on the street.

The street is steep, a street where everyone knows everyone else's business. The side opposite the salon is lined with offices and a couple of Indian trading stores, one of which Avril, five going on fifty years old, a real little mother hen, would toddle down to with a hand broom in one hand and a dustpan in the other. The Indian Mama, sitting crossed legged on the counter, as Indian Mama's do in trading stores, looks down on Avril with an unsmiling face, a suspicious face. Beady eyes follow every movement of this strange child who sweeps her floor. Not a word is exchanged by either of them.

Our side of the street has the George & Dragon, a bar commonly referred to as the G&D, at the top end. Mom's salon, Pamela's, abuts the shared courtyard with the G&D. Below Pamela's is a dress shop and below that an Indian tailor shop at the bottom. The tailor would usually be furiously pedaling his Singer sewing machine on his verandah, running up cotton frocks and shirts.

Here languages and smells co-mingle: Hindu, Urdu, Chechewa, Portuguese and English, incense, Indian curry spices, strong body odour, and wafting perm lotion from Pamela's salon, ever present as are the beggars. A man with Elephantiasis, his huge leg stretched out in front of him, sits on the pavement.

"Don't stare," Mom says, "Poor bugger." This elephant man and a young boy with a crippled leg take up their positions on the street every day. It's said that parents break a child's ankle at birth so that the child can earn money begging. Some native men with bulges in their pants always fascinate me. It's said they tie a rock to their penises to stretch them. This is the weirdest thing I have ever heard, why would they want stretched penises?

Mom's salon is a place of much hustle and bustle. Her shop is conveniently located across the courtyard from the G&D where the goings on in the salon are clearly visible to anyone occupying any of its bar stools.

Warren sits on a bar stool there, at the G&D, whiskey-and-soda in hand, and glares across the courtyard, keeping tabs on Mom. She knows he doesn't like her working late but she can't say no to her clients. Besides, she needs the money. She is late paying bills again.

"Mom, he's coming and boy, does he look mad!"

She has just lowered the hairdryer on the last shampoo-and-set for the day. There are another two ladies under dryers who need to be brushed out.

"Don't these bitches have homes to go to?" Warren yells as he storms through the door, glowering at the startled women.

"Please, don't do this, Warren," Mom begs.

"Is everything okay, Pamela?" one of the women asks.

"Yes, dear," Mom shouts under the dryer, patting the woman on the shoulder. "Everything is fine, dear."

"Everything is not fine. I said, *don't you bitches have homes to go to!*"

"What is he saying, Pamela? He looks mad." The women, clearly frightened now, see only Warren's contorted angry face. The drone of the hair dryers, mercifully garble his words.

"It's okay dear, he always looks like that," throwing Warren her narrow-eyed look "He just wants to know how much longer I will be." Please, go along with this her eyes plead of Warren.

"NO, I said . . . ."

"Come on Warren, let Mom finish, she's nearly done." I herd him out the door and back to his bar stool, knowing there will be hell to pay later. There always is. And there was.

It's another day now, another busy day in Pamela's Salon, but now there is time for me to hang out the window. Which I do just in time it seems, to see the sheriff's lorry turn at the top of the street. We hate that sheriff. He has no heart.

The sheriff's lorry, barreling down the hill to stop outside the salon was a familiar and dreaded sight. "Mom, the sheriff is here."

"Oh no!" Mom wails.

There are three ladies sitting under dryers and one hooked up to the permanent wave machine, wires attached to each curler on her head like some sort of brain monitoring equipment.

The sheriff marches in, bringing his stern face with him, a face that shows no compassion, no mercy and certainly no smile. His two sheepish assistants are close behind. They know the drill.

"Please, Sheriff, I mailed a cheque today," Mom says.

"Sorry, too late, I've come to repossess your machines."

He yanks the cords out of the wall, lifts the dryers off the heads of Mom's clients and rolls them towards his skivvies. He doesn't seem to know what to do about the brain machine, so he leaves it still attached to the lady emanating perm lotion fumes. "Take these to the lorry," he tells his assistant.

"You awful man, you should be ashamed of yourself," Mom says following her dryers to the door. She knows she's lost this battle, so she doesn't mind telling him he is awful, which of course he is.

She will have to call Leonard Thorne. He always gets them back for her somehow.

"Just doing my job," the sheriff says grimly.

"Yes, but you enjoy being a bully, don't you?" He doesn't answer. He's gone deaf.

The hairdryers are loaded onto the bed of the sheriff's lorry and off they go, rocking and rolling down the hill.

Sympathizers, with elbows on window ledges, chins on fists and bums in the air, comment to each other. "Poor Pamela, there go her hairdryers again."

"How is she supposed to run her business without her hairdryers?"

"*They* don't care, do they? The sods."

We drag the chairs out to the courtyard where the ladies' hair can dry in the sun. We settle them down with magazines, tea and Bakers lemon cream biscuits.

"Another cup of tea, dear?" Mom asks.

Suddenly, their hair day has turned into a tea party. Now they talk about the sheriff's awfulness. Stoic they are against this common enemy. One never knows what might happen at Pamela's Salon.

The time before the sheriff had come, Mom had been doing the Governor's wife's hair. "What does Pamela owe?" she asks the sheriff, pulling her chequebook out of her handbag. He tells her, and she writes out a cheque, handing it to him with a dismissive flourish.

It was no wonder our poor mother couldn't pay her bills. She gives no thought to doling out money from her till for anything Peter, Michael or I wanted. Or, for anyone else for that matter.

She had been doing the Governor's wife's hair on another occasion when the Governor himself walked in. This was unusual, as a chauffeur normally picked Mrs. Governor up.

"Pamela," the Governor asks, "do you think you could give me a quick trim? My barber is away,"

"Of course, Governor," says she who can never say "no." It was early, so I guess she figured she could finish before Warren turned up at the G & D.

That particular day, however, Warren had taken up his position on the bar stool earlier than usual. Glancing over at the salon, he sees Mom cutting the Governor's hair. He slams his whiskey on the counter and charges over to the salon.

"*Pamela*," he blusters, apoplectic over this blatant disregard for his rules, "I have told you – how many times have I told you? You are NOT ALLOWED to cut men's hair!"

Mom gives him one of her slitty-eyed looks, the one that scares us kids but doesn't scare Warren. Not one bit. "Warren, *this* is the Governor."

"I don't care if it's the bloody King of England. He's a man, isn't he?"

"It's okay, Pamela, I'll get my barber to finish up my hair when he gets back. Really, don't worry."

"No, Governor, I will finish cutting your hair. You can't possibly walk around like this." Mom sends another narrow look in Warrens direction, "We don't want the *Governor* walking around with half a haircut, do we, Warren? Of course we . . . ."

BANG. Warren slaps the scissors out of Mom's hand. Those scissors, now a silver missile, fly spread-eagled and twirling across the room. Clatter.

Clunk. Miraculously missing the Governor's wife, they land on the floor at her feet.

He shoots out of the chair, the Governor does, his cutting-cloak still around his shoulders. Out the door he scuttles, Mistress Governor hot on his tail. No backward glance from those two.

Warren slams his fist into Mom's face, once, twice. Blood runs into her eye from a split on her eyebrow. Blood drips onto her chest from her nose.

"Leave my mother alone, you bastard, you coward," I scream into Warren's face, my nose an inch from his chin.Warren grimaces, gives me a hateful look, turns, walks across the courtyard. "That's right you coward, go back to your bloody whiskey," I shout at his back.

"Mom, I don't understand why you want to stay with that man. I hate him. I HATE him. I wish he would die. Just die."

"Get me a wet towel, Rosebud. I suppose that's the last I'll see of the Governor's wife."

Crying hysterically now, Mom makes her way to a chair in a cubicle.

"Look what he has done to your face Mom. Just look at you."

"I know, I know. But no more, Rosebud. This is it, the end of it. I promise."

"I've heard that story before Mom. I hope you mean it this time. He's a coward and a bully. If he comes back in here I'm going to call the police."

"You know that does no good. They just say they can't get involved because it's a domestic issue."

"Well it is, as long as you live with him."

Mom has a broken nose, again. Of course, the Governor's wife comes back. Where else can she go?

The only other salon in Blantyre is really bad. Besides, she has an investment in this business, doesn't she?

Mom ends up with stitches in her eyebrow, a black eye and a white plaster over her nose. She tells her ladies that she ran into a glass door. They don't believe her.

We have to continue living in Warren's house until Mom can find another place to live. She is looking for a rental and I am hopeful.

A week later I happen to look out the window and see the Thorne's big old blue Humber pull up to the pavement. I should say it floated to the curb because that is just what that car did – it floated up, down, up, down, undulating over invisible bumps. Over real bumps, almost becoming airborne. Billie named it The Blue Peril. Aptly named to all who knew what travelled within.

Naturally, Billie, being an alcoholic had to be chauffeur-driven everywhere by her faithful driver and self-appointed guardian, Spade. Spade, a very proper black man in his forties, wore his spotless khaki uniform and cap with pride. He was fiercely loyal to Billie.

"Mom, the Blue Peril is here," I called.

"Oh, Billie doesn't have an appointment. Rosebud, see if you can bring her inside. She must *not* go into the G&D." Billie is blacklisted from most of the bars in town and the G&D is one of them.

I walk down the stairs to fetch Billie, but I don't see her. Where is she? She's not sitting in the Blue Peril. And why is Spade staring straight ahead? Why won't he look at me? Why doesn't he greet me?

The reason for this odd behavior is lying on the back seat, stark naked.

Billie, with her hanging breasts and sagging flesh is out cold, her mouth open, snoring. Poor old Billie (everyone prefaced Billie with *poor old*). She would eventually break out in abscesses with holes large enough to insert a fist, abscesses caused by alcohol poisoning. But that would be later.

I fetch Mom and we wrap Billie in cutting cloaks from the salon. With Spade's help, we get her into a back cubicle. Poor Spade. This dignified man is overwhelmed with embarrassment. He won't meet our eyes. "If that poor fellow could use his name to dig a hole to crawl into, he would," Mom says with a chuckle.

Mom calls Leonard at his Law Office. He asks her to keep Billie in the salon since he is unable to pick her up for a couple of hours: "And for god's sake don't let her get her hands on any booze."

Mom and I ignore Billie's many requests for whiskey and milk. Instead we ply her with coffee. Billie cries a lot about her own Rosemary, a daughter of hers in England with whom she is estranged. Why? We don't know but whenever she gets maudlin she tells me I remind her of her Rosemary.

A week before I'm to return to Bulawayo Betty Peterson, a regular client of Mom's invites us to her house on a tea estate. We sit on her long, deep, shaded verandah, overlooking manicured lawns, tea plantations and Mount Mulanje on the horizon, where the sun is going down in a blaze of red, orange and yellow, capturing all three of us in its glory, for a while.

Betty looks at her watch. "It's 6 o'clock. Where is the house boy with the drinks trolley? I need a G & T, don't you, Pamela?"

"Oh yes, Betty, that sounds just the ticket."

"Did you see John with his new floozy last night? What he sees in her I don't know. She must have hidden charms," Betty said.

"Yes, my dear, hidden below her waist I think."

"Ha, ha."

"Poor Jane, she should kick the bugger out." This, from Mom, she who has a hard time kicking *her* buggers out.

"I would not put up with that from Dick. Speaking of Dick, he is on another business trip to Salisbury. Poor dear, he works so hard." Betty said.

"He spends a lot of time in Salisbury. Are you sure he doesn't have a floozy down there?" says Mom, sticking her neck out.

"Who, Dick? Good Lord no, he doesn't know what to do with that thing in his pants anymore."

"Another G & T, my dear?"

"I thought you would never ask."

She rings a bell.

"Inde, Dona."

"Bring some more ice, will you Joseph."

"Inde, Dona."

Mom was not usually one of these verandah sitters, at least not during the week. She was too busy working. But this is a Sunday and she had had a rough time last night by the looks of her today.

On Monday, while brushing out a clients' hair, Mom confides to her, "You know, Dick Peterson* has a floozy in Salisbury, don't you?"

"Really? Does Betty know?"

"No, my dear she is oblivious. She thinks his trips to Salisbury are for work. At least he isn't shitting on his own doorstep like John Henderson*. John is like the cat that crept into the crypt, crapped and crept out again."

"Poor Jane."

No one could tell a story quite like Mom could. She embellished where she thought fit. If she didn't know something, or, didn't like what she knew, well, she just changed it, making up a far more entertaining tale.

"When Mr. so and so walks out the front door to go to work, Mrs. so and so lets her lover, so and so, in the back door."

"Really?"

All this is another reason women loved to come to Pamela's Hairdressing Salon.

Another story Mom told, which would have her rapt audience in tears of laughter, was about the Major and "Bed Tea." Major Henderson, purportedly a remittance man from England, was referred to as Hendy or just Major. He earned his title from the Second World War. He was a confirmed bachelor. Mom would say, "He will never get married as no woman would put up with him." He lives on a small farm situated halfway between Blantyre and Zomba.

As the story goes, the Major was driving back to his farm from Blantyre one hot day when he sees a young lad hitch hiking on the side of the road. Pulling to a stop, he winds down his window,

"You must not be from around here, young man, or you would know you should be wearing a hat in this heat. Where are you going?"

"No, I'm not from here Sir, I'm with the American Peace Corps, and I have to report for the start of my two-year duty in Zomba. I couldn't find transportation, Sir so I'm walking to Zomba."

"You're in luck. Hop in, I'm going to the Zomba Club, but, if you don't mind, I have to stop at my farm first. Few things I have to take care of."

"Thank you, Sir."

The flushed, perspiring young man is grateful for the ride and to get out of the brutal sun. Indeed, it's his lucky day.

The Major's old brick and shingle roofed farmhouse has the usual verandah running its length. This is where the Major leaves the young man. He returns half an hour later with a bottle of gin, a bucket of ice and some tonics. "We'll have a snort before we leave."

Two days later, this poor young man, who probably had never had a drop of alcohol in his life, sports a two-day growth on his chin, a bewildered look on his face and reeks of gin. In a plaintive voice he begs: "Major, Sir, I really, really have to go to Zomba, Sir."

"Cookie," the major bellows.

"Yes, Bwana."

"Get your bicycle and take this Bwana to Zomba."

"To Zomba, Bwana?" Zomba is a long way away.

"Yes, to Zomba."

"Inde, Bwana."

Precariously perched on the carrier of Cookie's bike, hanging on for dear life, the drunken young man must not have felt lucky anymore. Off they go, wobbling down the dirt, corrugated road at an alarming speed. They have a lot of miles to cover.

What happened to that young man? It's thought that he is sent back to America, thoroughly disgraced, having been corrupted in the tropics and ruing the day he accepted a lift from the Major.

There was another story bandied about in bars and Pamela's Hairdressing Salon. All expats had servants, and most were served what was called "bed tea" early each morning. Expats are enticed to Nyasaland, mainly from England, to work for the government. These are desirable jobs and usually come with a generous, three-month leave package "back-home," a free house and servants. The servants were usually inherited from the retiring, hard drinking, tropically corrupted government worker, who was going back home for good.

One such import to the Public Works Department was a new District Commissioner. His first morning in his newly inherited house, he is awoken by the sound of his bedroom door slowly squeaking open. Shuffle, shuffle, feet cross the highly polished wood floor. Slightly alarmed, he lay stock-still. Peeping from one eye he watches as his inherited servant lifts his mosquito net. A black finger reaches for his eyelid, lifts it, gently replaces it. Shuffle, shuffle, door opens, door closes.

Fifteen minutes later, he hasn't moved. He is puzzled. Door opens, Shuffle, shuffle. His servant has returned with a cup of bed tea. He knows everyone gets bed tea in the morning, but lifting the eyelid! What odd behavior.

This ritual is repeated for the next couple of mornings. Is this some strange African custom that no one told him about, he wonders? On the third morning, the Commissioner sits down to his breakfast as usual. "Moni, Bambo."

"Moni, Bwana."

"Tell me, Bambo, why do you do that strange thing in the morning?"

"What strange thing, Bwana?"

"You come into my room every morning, lift my eyelid, then put it back down, then you go out and bring me tea. Are you trying to see if I am awake?"

"Ah that. Well, Sah, the last Bwana before you, he teach me this thing. He say, in the morning I must lift his eye. If his eye is white, then I must bring him tea. If it is red I must bring him coffee and aspirins."

"Aaah!" stifling laughter the commissioner says. "Well, it's not necessary to do that for me Bambo. Just bring me tea every morning."

Natives were extremely tolerant of the white man's behavior and foibles, no matter how odd. Almost like indulgent parents, they took it in their stride. Often, though, what one said was taken quite literally.

Ever since the Governor incident, with my constant prodding, Mom has been looking for a place to rent. A large flat, steps from the salon becomes available, Mom snatches it up and we move out of Warren's house. Warren is not completely out of the picture, but I am hopeful he will be soon. At least Mom is not living in his house anymore.

The holidays are almost over and in a few days, I have to get back on that big old Dakota and fly back to Bulawayo. I hate to think about going back to Rumble Bum, to school, to the Longdrop, and I especially hate to leave Mom.

RUMBLE BUM IS LEFT TO RUMBLE ON HIS OWN

In the middle of the night, we are awakened by screaming. We all know what is happening, again, and we leap out of our beds and run out the door.

They tumble, Uncle Ernie and Aunt Patty, then roll out of their room. He is punching her. She crawls into the kitchen. He jumps on her back, pulls her head up by her hair with his left hand and slams his right fist into the side of her head.

The closest weapon to me is a heavy beer tankard. I pick it up and hit Uncle Ernie on the head with it as hard as I can. Irene stabs him in the back with a fork. The prongs sink into his flesh. Uncle Ernie lets Aunt Patty's head fall to the floor with a thud and lunges for Irene. I stand there, mesmerized by that fork in his back, staring at it as it moves up and down with his panting. It wobbles for a second or two before it falls to the kitchen floor with a clatter that snaps me out of my trance and I wobble too, a little shocked that I have actually hit Rumble Bum on the head with his own beer tankard. Now that the fork has fallen, blood bubbles out the four holes made by the fork and trickles down his back.

Uncle Ernie has Irene by the neck. I pound his back with the beer tankard, but he pays no attention to me. It's Irene he wants to choke. It's always Irene.

"Ernie," Aunt Patty shrieks, "let her go! Let her go! You'll kill her."

He lets her go with a push. "Get out! Get out of my house," he bellows.

Blue faced, Irene runs out the door, gulping for air. Aunt Patty and the rest of us run into our bedroom, slam the door, barricade it. Everyone is howling except me. I'm not crying, I'm shaking and breathing hard, worrying about Irene. I must find her.

Grabbing two pillows and a blanket off the bed, I jump out the window. I couldn't possibly sleep in a bed while Irene is outside in the dark somewhere.

It doesn't take long to find her, partly from guessing and partly because of her wheezing. She is on the carport roof, having an asthma attack, a bad one, the worst I have ever seen her have. She sits up there, on that roof, rocking back and forth, gasping for air, her throat making awful rasping noises.

I throw the pillows, one by one, up and onto the roof, then the blanket. After that I climb the tree alongside the carport and jump down onto the iron roof.

"Rene. Rene, are you going to be okay?" I'm so scared for her.

She just nods her head and slices the air with her hand. We sit like that for a long time, until her breathing becomes easier.

"How did you know where I was?" she asks.

"The wheezing."

"I hate him so much, Rosebud."

"I know Rene, I know you do."

With our heads on the pillows and our bodies covered by the old threadbare blanket, we stare at the night sky threaded with stars, stars that speckle and sparkle, sending points of twinkling light down to us. Then we see it, the shooting star, as it streaks across the sky. "Make a wish, make a wish," we whisper in unison.

This theatre in the sky distracts us as we try to ignore the corrugations of that iron roof under our backs. "How can there be so much bad stuff under these beautiful stars, Rosebud?"

"I don't know, Rene. Perhaps God has put the stars in the sky to show us there is good stuff too."

"Hmmmm . . . I don't believe in God anymore."

"Nor do I really. If there is one, a God that is, he must be deaf and blind, too."

We listen to the crickets, crrrrk, crrrrrk and the ribit, ribit, ribit of the frogs for a while as we ponder this enigma.

"We could run away you know, Rene. You are sixteen. You could get a job."

"But what about Mom? I couldn't leave Mom with him. He'll kill her one day."

"What about you Rene? Your father will kill you one day."

"I'll kill him first," she says with utter conviction.

Irene is one of the bravest, feistiest, people I know.

The two of us lie there on that hard roof until the moon and sun trade places. Then we sneak back to the bedroom before Uncle Ernie comes for his car.

Aunt Patty can't go to work today because she looks so bad, and Irene and I are too tired to go to school. We stay in bed while Aunt Patty goes to see a doctor. When she comes back she tells us what a lovely man the doctor is. He had been appalled by her beating, and urges her to leave Uncle Ernie, if not for her own sake then at least for Irene's sake. He also tells her she deserves a man who will kiss her from head to toe every day, as he does *his* wife. Aunt Patty thinks this is the loveliest thing she has ever heard, and I think from that moment on she fantasized about meeting a man who would love her in this fashion.

Aunt Patty has a broken eardrum along with a damaged tear duct, bruises and a bald spot on her head where Uncle Ernie pulled a handful of hair out. Irene has blue finger marks on her neck that will, in a few days, go yellow and brown before disappearing.

We need to disappear.

Aunt Patty would always say, "He's your father, Irene, don't be cheeky to him." Now she thinks it's better for Irene to have no father, better for all the kids, really. Surely no father would be better than the violent one Rumble Bum has become.

Aunt Patty tells Irene and me that she is making plans for us to leave Uncle Ernie. "I'm working on it," she says, "Aunt Polly left us a little money. We'll use that to move. I promise you, Irene, we will move away."

Poof!

We'll just vanish. Just like that. Just like Great Aunt-Polly. We are so happy with this thought.

True to her word, Aunt Patty finds us a house a hundred miles away, in Gwelo. Uncle Peter Foster brings his lorry and a big trailer to the farm. He helps us pack up while Uncle Ernie is at work. We leave with all our boxes of clothes and three single beds.

We don't need much because the house in Gwelo is furnished. We kids, all five of us, are in the bed of the lorry, tucked into niches here and there, with the boxes and two Ridgebacks.

The cow is in the trailer. Uncle Peter had said, "You are not taking the cow are you, Patty?"

"Of course I am, Peter, I would never leave my cow."

Uncle Peter laughs so hard he has to hold his stomach, "We're going to look like a bunch of jaapies," he splutters. Jaapies, pronounced Yaahpeas, is what the English call Afrikaners.

Aunt Patty would never leave her beloved cow behind, never. We knew that. Besides, we all need her milk and though I don't know it yet, I need her dung. So off we go, cow and all, to Gwelo.

There is no going back, Aunt Patty says. This is it. No going back. We have taken the go-away-bird's advice.

Gleefully we imagine Rumble Bum's shock when he gets home to find us gone, gone, gone. What a delicious picture this is for us on that long uncomfortable trek. We are sad though, to be leaving Nyama. At least he has a nice new kaia now. My cousin Reggie, Sambo, as Uncle Ernie called him, is the only one sad to be leaving his Dad.

The house we are going to belongs to another uncle, Uncle Donald MacDonald. This had all been arranged before we left Bulawayo. When we get there, we are so excited because not only is it a big house where Irene and I each have our own rooms, but it has an inside toilet. Yipeeee! No more Longdrop. And there are taps to give us hot water for baths. What luxury. Voetsek, Longdrop. Voetsek, Rumble Bum.

It's so peaceful and Aunt Patty plays her music, Richard Tauber, Mario Lanza and Caruso, on her phonograph, without Rumble Bum's complaining. Aunt Patty starts her new job as a bookkeeper with a tombstone manufacturing company, aptly named Graves & Son. Pty. Ltd.

Mom sends money for school uniforms for everyone. This probably means her hairdryers will be repossessed again, rudely pulled out of the wall plugs, by that awful sheriff.

Chaplin High is my new school. I would soon come to hate it. I am fifteen and Irene is sixteen. Irene will be going to the convent school. She has decided she wants to be a nun, an ambition I could not understand.

MONKEYS UP A TREE AND SKIN LIKE A BABY'S BOTTOM

Mr. Fitzgerald is my arithmetic teacher at Chaplin High. He seems amused that we have the same surname. Arithmetic is not one of my strong subjects, so Mr. Fitzgerald takes me with him to other, lower forms, where I sit during his lesson on a chair at his desk. I am humiliated. I hate being singled out. He may as well have put a dunce cap on my head. I don't study for the up-coming test and when it is over, I know I have flunked it. I just hope not badly enough to send me onto my desk.

"Monkeys up a tree," Mr. Fitzgerald bellows.

Oh No!

Oh yes.

His finger is trained on me. There is no point in bluffing that it could be for someone behind me. There is no one behind me; mine is the last desk at the back of the classroom.

This is a good thing if you have to get on your desk. No one can see the back of your legs. It's a bad thing if you want to pretend the finger is not for you.

"Yes, you Rosemary, you, Monkeys Up A Tree," Mr. Fitzgerald says.

Is that a smile on his face? No, it's a smirk. He loves to embarrass me. I know he does.

There is nothing else for me to do but get up there on my desk. So, I do and I stand on it like a fool. My cheeks are red-hot. I wish something catastrophic would happen, something like a meteor hitting the building. Then I can sneak out while Mr. Fitzgerald is attending to the injured. But I know the only thing that will be injured today is my pride.

Some students snicker as he goes over the sums I got wrong in the test. I know their turn will come sooner or later, but I won't be here to snicker at them, because I am not going to be at this school for long. That is what I decide as I stand there, on my desk.

I hate arithmetic almost as much as I hate Mr. Fitzgerald. I don't like that he has the same surname as I do, either. I take my mind out of that classroom as I stand up here on this desk. Take it to the Friday night hop Irene and I went to last week.

With our felt skirts, (which Mom made for us) layers of starched petticoats, white socks and wide elastic belts cinching our waists, we walked into the hall with our pony tails swishing and bouncing. Oh boy, we thought we were hot.

Bill Haley was singing, *Rock around the Clock*. Chairs lined the walls and trestle tables were laid out with snacks and sodas. Balloons and crepe paper decorations hang from the ceiling. Irene and I had been practicing dancing with our doorknobs for weeks. Now we were ready to show off our dancing.

"Pssst! Rene, look at that mush guy over there, across the room." He was dressed in black, slouching up against the wall. His thick black hair, Elvis style, hung over one eye. He wore a crooked smirk, not unlike Mr. Fitzgerald's smirk.

"He's looking at you, Bud." He was! Looking me up and down. He didn't looked away, either, when our eyes met.

Slowly he'd sauntered over to me. Saunter is the only way to describe the way he came over and stood in front of me. My heart nearly jumped out of my chest when he asked me to dance. *Don't Be Cruel* was now blaring out of speakers in each corner of the dance hall.

That's it! I'm in love. Well, I think it's love because my stomach feels like jelly. I find out that he is my fifth cousin removed, Rory MacDonald, Uncle Donald's son and that he lives next door to us! What luck.

Rory was always leaning up against something, or sleeping. His father says he is lazy, Aunt Patty says he has bilharzia from swimming in the rivers. I say bilharzia or no bilharzia, lazy or not, in my opinion he is the bee's knees. He asks me to go steady.

"Rosemary you can get down from your desk now." Mr. Fitzgerald's voice snaps me out of my reverie.

I do come down from my desk and run past him, right past him, without even saying goodbye.

It's a long weekend, Guy Fawkes Day is on Monday and Peter is picking me up from school. He is visiting us in Gwelo for the weekend. He is so handsome and all of a sudden I'm very popular with the snickering, snooty girls from my class. "Is *that* your brother?" "Yeah." Yawn. Pride bursts through my ribs, sending shards of bone into the eyes of the girls who usually ignore me and who are now falling over themselves to talk to me. "He is *so* good-looking. Has he got a girlfriend?"

"I dunno. Who cares?" Yawn.

Tee Hee.

On the way home Peter says, "Rosebud, do you want skin like a baby's bottom?"

"Yes." Of course, I want skin like a baby's bottom.

"Well you know what you have to do?"

"What?"

"You have to put cow dung on your face."

"EEYU!"

"There's nothing wrong with dung, its only grass. It has to be fresh and warm though, and you have to let it dry on your face before you wash it off. You'll have skin like a baby's bottom, I promise."

When the cow dumps a fresh patty, I smear it on my face. As the dung dries to a brown-yellow mask on my face, my skin starts to prickle. Then it starts to burn. Then it's on fire. "Peter, it's burning! My face is burning. Can I wash the dung off now?"

"Ach man, don't be a sissy. That means it's working, leave it on. It's not dry enough yet."

I walk in circles, moaning, "It feels like a swarm of bees are stinging my face, Peter,"

"Good, good, it's supposed to." He says again, "I promise, you'll have skin like a baby's bottom when you wash it off."

But what about the bees? The crawling, stinging bees on my face, what about them? "Ohhh! I can't stand it any longer Peter. I can't stand it!"

BANG. The bathroom door slams against the wall with the force of my shove in my desperation to reach water. Then it bounces back, the door, and hits me in the face. It feels good, that door hitting me in the face. The pain of it makes my eyes water, my nose burn, for just a minute I forget about the stinging bees as my tears soak into the dung forging dark runnels down my cheeks. With a mad dash I run to the bath, turn on the cold tap and splash my face with the soothing water.

Lumps of dung fall to the tub bottom. Plop. Plop.

Cow poop stops up the plughole and the bath fills with water, brown floating lumps swirl dangerously close to the rim of the tub.

I don't care.

All I care about now is the tomato that stares back at me from the mirror. A bright red tomato it is, with thick hot tears forging down its plumpness, or is that blood?

I think its blood!

"Peter my face is bleeding," I scream.

Peter comes into the bathroom to inspect my face.

"Ach man, it's not bleeding, it's just red like it's supposed to be."

I slather handfuls of Vaseline all over my face. *AAAAh!* Finally, the bees leave. But the angry red tomato stays. It stays for quite a while, trying to burst out of its skin and it throbs with a dull ache.

"It's the ammonia in the cow dung." Aunt Patty explains, "Rosebud, you are too gullible. Why do you take your brothers so seriously? Anyway, you have beautiful skin for goodness sake."

It takes about a week for the fissures to appear. My face looks like the parched earth in the bush veldt.

The cracks open and in another week, I am able to peel the skin off my face in sheaths.

Indeed I do have skin like a baby's bottom, albeit a bright pink bottom.

Peter leaves, with all his bright ideas, to join Mom in Nyasaland. And I have to go back to school and Mr. Fitzgerald.

Or not?

Aunt Patty finds me curled up on a tombstone. She had taken some customers out to the yard to look at headstones and there I am fast asleep on a tombstone in the sun when I should have been at school. Playing truant again, only this time, I had fallen asleep on the job. "I hate school Aunt Patty, and I hate that Irish teacher, Mr. Fitzgerald."

"Rosebud, you have to finish school."

"I'm *not* going to be a monkey up a tree again, ever, ever! I don't care what happens. No more monkeys up a tree."

That's when I really start nagging Mom and Aunt Patty. I pout, I whine, I cry, I even beg. Finally, after pulling every trick I can think of I pull out the *big* one, the one I'd been saving as a last resort. "Mom," I say into the telephone, "If you don't let me leave school I'm going to run away, I will. I promise you, I will, Mom, and you will never find me."

"Oh, for crying in a bucket, Rosebud, leave then." Finally, I had worn her down.

And I do leave. At sixteen, I just stop going to school.

Rumble Bum shows up one Saturday. How did he find out where we live? He came to ask Aunt Patty to come back to the farm. With our ears pressed to the closed door, Irene and I hear Aunt Patty tell him, "Ernie, I should have left you the first time you put your hands on me. Beating me is one thing, but Irene? No Ernie, you went too far when you started on Irene. It's over Ernie, I want a divorce."

"Well, you're not going to get one from me." He says, "I'll see you in hell first." At least he knows *he* is going to hell.

I get a job in Pickering's Chemist. Though I am sixteen, I look much older. I am to work the counter, the cash register and restocking the back storeroom. I feel so grown up – that is, until Mr. Pickering pinches my nipple one day in the stock room.

He is a skinny man. Everything about him is skinny. Skinny hair, combed over his almost-bald head, from a parting just over his left ear, this drape sometimes flops down and hangs almost to his left shoulder, before he sweeps it back and over his head. Skinny lips, round wire glasses. Not only is he skinny, he is grey too, grey hair, grey eyes, grey skin. Grey-skinny-mr-pickering.

He had come into the stock room so quietly I didn't know he was behind me until he'd reached over my shoulder, grabbed my right boob and pinched my nipple, right through my bra! My 38 D bra holds my large breasts and my shame.

Pinched my nipple!

My face burns. My ears roar. I drop the box of vials I was loading onto the shelf and dart past him to the front of the shop, taking my red face and my nipple that still feels his pinch, to the stool at the end of the counter.

Now what? Should I leave? No, I'll just sit here and not look at him. I think I'm going to cry. I need to leave. Yes, I'll just go.

I pick up my handbag and wobble towards the door… "Rosemary, don't…" The door, closing behind me, swallows the rest of his sentence.

"You are not going back there," Aunt Patty says.

"But what about my salary?"

"You leave that to me."

The next morning, oblivious to customers, Aunt Patty storms into Pickering's, stands at the counter, slaps it, slaps it again. Through the plate glass window, from a safe place on the pavement, I see Mr. Pickering's hands begin to shake. I actually feel quite sorry for him

He is scared. More than scared, he is terrified. His grey face turns white. The two customers in the shop stare, mouths agape, from Aunt Patty to him, from him to Aunt Patty.

Mr. Pickering's shaky hands reach into the till to withdraw a stack of notes, he counts bills into Aunt Patty's out-stretched hand, stops, looks at Aunt Patty, who shakes her head. He reaches back into the till for more money, counts it, places it in her hand. With that Aunt Patty turns, says something over her shoulder, leaves.

"Come on, Rosebud." Aunt Patty, her head high, takes me by the elbow.

"What happened? What happened Aunt Patty?"

"He just counted out your salary and when he thought he was done, I told him he wasn't. What about her two weeks' notice, I said? He couldn't count more money out fast enough." Aunt Patty, laughs and dabs at the corner of her eye with a tissue, the eye with the Rumble Bum damaged tear duct.

"What did you say to him, when you left?"

"I asked him whether he would like me to tell his wife that he grabbed my niece's breast and pinched her nipple."

"Then what, then what?"

"Oh, I asked him what gave him the idea that he could have a chance with my beautiful niece and I told him he is a dirty little man."

I push this rather unfortunate event from my mind and hope I never have to see Mr. Pickering again.

LOVE IS A MANY SPLINTERED THING

Love is tragic, it's drama, it hurts. That's what I have learnt.

You love your mother and father. You love your brothers and sisters. You love lots of people that way, the way you love them, don't you? But are *you* lovable? How can you be? What Henry, mom's boyfriend in Salisbury, did to you made you dirty. You don't love Henry, you don't like Henry. In fact you hate Henry, so why did his hand arouse something in you? Give you a feeling that you had no control over? That is dirty. Isn't it? You can take *that* you away. And you do. You pretend you are lovable. Pretend you are Fancy or Scarlet O'Hara or any tragic, lovable creature on celluloid film. You hurt the one who loves you and love the one who hurts you.

That's what Mom does.

All this is proven when Rory takes me to see the film: *Love is a Many Splendored Thing*. Now I'm Jennifer Jones and I cry, and I hurt, and my heart is broken. That butterfly at the end, it's just too overwhelmingly sad.

"It's only a film, Rosebud, it's not real." Aunt Patty says.

"It's not just a film, it's a true story."

"It is?"

"Yes. Yes, it is."

It won't leave my mind, this fateful film. I dissolve into tears, over and over, for weeks. And then one night I am with Rory and I am Jennifer Jones. I'm enchanting, mesmerizing, passionate and tragic. Then all of a sudden, I don't want to look at him again. Ever. Rory is not William Holden. I tell him I don't want to see him anymore and I ignore him when I do.

Where is that go-away-bird?

Mom is still the worry that gnaws at my stomach, Dad the pain that tugs at my heart, and Henry the shame I guard possessively. It's mine after all, all mine. I shove that shame into the back seat where I can warily watch it in the rear-view mirror. Sometimes it would force its way into the front seat, or even the driver's seat, if I'm not vigilant, if I let my guard down over some capricious distraction.

I fly back to Nyasaland.

The good news is that Warren is out of the picture for good now.

The bad news is that Joe Darrach, a stocky ex-boxer from Ireland, with the scars of his old profession on his face, is the new star on Mom's screen. Ruggedly handsome, Joe would be rugged on Mom, adding to the scars Warren had left on her face. I realize that Boxer Joe is worse, far worse, than Warren.

Late one night, I see Joe come out of Avril's bedroom. I confront him. "What were you doing in there?"

"Just checking on her," he says.

"What do you mean, checking on her? You have no business being in my sister's room."

I call out to her, "Avey, are you okay?" She is crying but she insists she's okay, I don't believe her, and I yell for Peter. He comes stumbling out of his bedroom, all rumpled and sleepy eyed.

"What? What's going on? Why is Avril crying?"

"I don't know Peter, but I saw Joe come out of her bedroom."

"You *what*? Where is he? Where is that bastard?"

"I think he's going to the G&D, Peter."

With that Peter dashes out the door in his pajama pants that have a big tear in the back showing his bum. I'm hot on his heels. Peter rugby tackles Joe. They both fall to the ground and punches fly.

"My balls! Let go of my balls you bastard." Peter screams.

"Leave my brother alone, you bully." I shout.

Mom has come out now in her nightdress, screaming at Peter and Joe to "*Stop it!*"

A small crowd from the bar gathers around, adding to the confusion.

"Jesus Christ, my ear, you bit my ear, you little shit." Joe yells.

"You want to fight dirty, Joe, I can too."

Peter had bitten a piece out of Boxer Joe's ear. Blood runs down his neck. Mom and I drag Peter away while the bar crowd holds onto Joe.

Avril insists he didn't hurt her. She says she got a fright when she woke up to see him sitting on her bed. Joe later insists he didn't do anything to her. Mom believes him. I don't. He's back in the fold and I hate him more than ever. I refuse to acknowledge his presence.

A couple of weeks later, Mom comes into my room, with a cigarette wedged between her thumb and forefinger. "What are you doing with that?" I ask her.

"I found it in my vagina this morning"

"You what?"

"It was sticking out of my fanny. Joe must have put it there when I was sleeping."

"Why? Why would he do that?"

"You know how he hates smoking. I smoked a cigarette at the bar last night."

"Really, Mom, you don't even know how to smoke."

"I didn't inhale."

"Mom, why do you do stuff to antagonize him? You know he hates smoking."

"He was just annoying me, being mean to me."

"Well you got the rise out of him you wanted, didn't you? Anyway, you should have booted him out after the fight."

"Rosebud, he didn't do anything to Avril. Peter over-reacted."

"No, Peter didn't, he was protecting his little sister and you, Mom, should have backed him up. Believe what you want to believe. I'm glad Peter bit his earlobe off."

I hadn't given Rory a single thought since I left Gwelo, so you can imagine my surprise when I come home from the salon and see him sitting in our lounge, lounging in our lounge, like a lizard.

"What are you doing here," I rudely ask him.

"I've come to see Mick and Peter…and, you," he says with a sheepish grin.

He has no job and no money. He hangs around. I ignore him.

"Shame, Rosebud," Mom says "Don't be mean to Rory. He's so in love with you."

"Well, I don't want him to be. I just want him to leave, to go away."

At night Rory lies on the half-wall below my window and whistles. Nonstop. It drives me crazy. "Go away, Rory! Go away and stop that bloody whistling."

"How can you be so cruel?" Mom says, "Why are you so cruel to him, Rosebud?"

"Because he's not William Holden."

"What? What's that got to do with the price of cheese?"

"Everything."

Uncle Donald sends Rory an air ticket and he goes back to Gwelo. I go back to trying not to feel bad and guilty when I think about him.

After Rory, I meet a man 13 years older than me. We met in the courtyard outside the G&D. Mom cannot stand him and she forbids me to see him. I sneak out and meet him and when I get home Mom and I have a big fight. His name is Henry and he is a bricklayer from South Africa. Mom says he is a deadbeat. She says he has no business trying to date a 16-year-old girl. She doesn't know the only reason I came home at all tonight was to get some clothes. Because I'm going to run away with Henry Heidenrach – that is what I have decided.

"You've been drinking, Rosebud."

"Of course, I have. It's the fashion around here. Monkey do what monkey see."

"He is much too old for you. He has a bad reputation."

"So, show me someone with a good reputation around here."

"Don't be cheeky to your mother."

"I'm going to see him whether you like it or not, Mom."

"I will call your father."

"Oh, so now he's my father? Dad is my father when it suits you!"

"Rosebud, if you leave, I'll kill myself. I will, I swear to God."

"Sorry, Mom, that won't work tonight. Bye."

"Rosebud, Rosebud, come…"

Slam. The door shuts out the rest of Mom's words. I take the stairs, two at a time. Henry's Volvo is running, the passenger door open, I leap into the seat, slam the door shut and we pull off with tyres screeching.

My blood pumps in my veins. I'm scared. I'm elated. I'm scared. I'm sad because I hurt Mom. I'm sad because I said awful, unkind things to her. Sad because I know she will be sad, too, when she realizes I'm never coming back, ever. That I have gone forever.

Forever was not going to be very long. In fact, forever lasted only about three hours. "Henry, didn't you say your friend Brian is having a party tonight?"

"Yeah, want to go?"

"Yes."

It's a raucous party, people coming and going. Henry and I are dancing when I feel the tap on my shoulder. I swing around.

"Rosemary, we've come to get you." It's the Chief of Police, Frank Chevalier, all decked out in his khaki uniform, a black leather strap running diagonally across his chest, badges, a gun and a stiff peak cap that matches his stiff upper lip.

Mom stands about twenty feet away. How did she know we were here? Did someone call her? "I'm not going with her, I hate her," I tell the Police Chief.

"Well, she loves you."

"No, she doesn't. She doesn't. If she loved me she would let me see Henry."

"Rosebud, come home, darling. You are making a big mistake," Mom butts in.

"I can arrest your friend here for kidnapping a minor. Would you like me to do that?" asks Mister Stiff Upper Lip.

"No."

"Then let me take you home."

"Rosebud, please darling. Come home."

"No, I want to go to Dad, I want Dad!"

"Okay, that's fine, I'll take you to your Dad," stiff Upper Lip says. He knows my dad. Everyone knows my Dad.

Except for me sniffling in the back seat there is silence all the way to Chigamula. When we get there, Dad opens the door in his pajamas. Aunt Rose and Cleone, Aunt Rose's 26-year-old daughter whom Dad is now engaged to, stand behind him, both of them with upper lips stiffer than the Police Chief's. Two holy chins in the air. I'm sure *they* will let me see Henry just because Mom won't. Cleone hates Mom because she always causes a scene if she and Dad happen to have the misfortune of being in the same place, like the club or a restaurant, where Mom is. But I am wrong.

"We'll talk about this in the morning, Rosebud," Dad says, patting my shoulder, "You go to sleep. It's after midnight."

In the morning I go to find Dad in his office, which is about a hundred yards from the house. Blubbering, I beg and plead with him to let me see Henry. "Please, please, please Dad, can he visit me here? We won't go out, please."

"Okay, okay," Dad, agrees.

"E-bloody-ikona," both Cleone and Aunt Rose say when I tell them Dad said Henry could visit me, "that man does not come onto this property. If he does we'll have him arrested." Have they been talking to Mom? With that they march up to Dad's office. "Gerry," they say, "what were you thinking? That man does not come onto this property." They're very cross with him. Poor Dad, he hates this kind of stuff, and I feel bad for getting him into trouble. All he wants is a peaceful life and I know what a softie he is when it comes to tears. I took advantage of that.

So that is it and I'm heartbroken.

Living at Chigamula, which is eight miles out of town, is boring, boring, boring. I tell Dad I want to go back to Mom. I think Cleone and Aunt Rose want me to go back to Mom too, and so Dad takes me back.

Henry, like the other Henry, is never seen or heard from again. Not by me anyway. He disappeared from Nyasaland and would soon disappear from my thoughts. Did they kill him? Ha! Ha! So much for love being everlasting. So much for love being a many-splendored thing.

It's more like a many-splintered thing, if you ask me.

HOGMANAY AND ROCK N' ROLL

The Limbe Country Club is holding its customary New Year's Eve dance and Peter and I are going. Mom starts sewing a dress for me at 4 p.m. and by 7 p.m. I walk out of the house wearing it.

The skirt has clouds and clouds of pale blue chiffon, a form-fitting bodice with shoestring straps. The satin pumps on my feet are dyed the same soft blue as my dress. The false nails I painstaking attached to each bitten-to-the-quick, ugly fingernail I painted bright, shiny red. They look fabulous and I keep looking at them.

How glamorous I feel tonight in this dress Mom made me. She had not had time to put a zip in the back, so she stitched it up on me. I am filled with delicious anticipation on the drive to the club. I have a crush on a boy called Gerry and I'm hoping he will be at the dance tonight. "Peter, do you think Gerry will be there?"

"I saw him yesterday and he said he was coming. You like him, don't you?" Peter asked.

"He's ok."

"Aw, come on Rosebud, admit it, you fancy him."

"No, I don't."

"Well, he fancies you."

"How do you know?"

"'Cause he asked me if you were coming tonight."

My tummy does flip-flops. "Doesn't mean he fancies me."

The smoke-filled hall is jammed. As we enter, we hear the sounds of laughter, clinking glasses, and *Blue Moon* by the Miracles. Dancers sway on the dance floor and I have a brandy and coke to give me courage. I hate walking into a room full of people. I always think everyone is looking at my breasts.

He's not here. I knew he wouldn't come. How stupid, how silly, to think he would.

THERE HE IS!! Looking oh so cool in his sports jacket and grey flannels. "Peter who is that girl Gerry is talking to?"

"How should I know? Never seen her before."

Hmmm!

"Think she's pretty?"

"She's okay, not as pretty as you."

"Really?"

"Yeah, you're much prettier than her."

"Oh! No! Here comes lumbering Brian. Save me Peter, let's dance."

"Uh uh, I want to find Sally."

"Please, please, Peter, I don't want to dance with him."

"Then don't."

"Dance?" Brian asks with his hand stretched out.

"Uh, uh…okay." Darn, why can't I ever say no? I'm just like Mom.

On the third agonizing song and dance with Brian, the music is interrupted. "Ladies and

Gentlemen, Peter and Rosemary Fitzgerald have agreed to Rock n' Roll for us tonight." Clap, clap, whistle, *schweeet*. Peter took it upon himself to agree for us to put on a show. I am mortified. "Come on Peter, come on Rosemary show us how it's done."

Peter looks just like his hero, Elvis, as he saunters over to me in his black shirt, black pants, white belt and white shoes. His hair is in a quaff which flops over one eye, a lob-sided grin on his handsome face. He knows I'm not amused.

You Aint Nothin But a Hound Dog starts to play.

We rock, rock, and rock. Peter signals for a roll. His face dripping, his hands wet, he rolls me over his back, pull, push, pull. His hands on my waist, he lifts me and brings me down, swish, between his legs and I slip right out of his sweaty clutches. Off I go skidding across the dance floor on my bum. Billows of blue chiffon float about my head like a fallen cloud. My face is hot.

"GET UP, get up," Peter snarls gyrating towards me on rubber legs "Pretend that was part of the act, come on, come on, get up"

"I. AM. TRYING. TO, PETER!" I'm also trying to untangle myself from all the chiffon that has engulfed me.

I wobble towards him. Hot, cold, hot, oh I ache, my body, my neck, my eyes, behind my eyes. I know this feeling. I've had it many times before, this aching in the marrow of my bones.

SCHWEET. The crowd whistles, stomp their feet. More! More! They yell. What good sports they are.

"*Don't Be Cruel* to a heart that's true," starts playing and we dance. I'm feeling really sick now.

Huffing, puffing, gasping, rocking and reeling, red finger nails falling like drops of blood all over the dance floor. Sticky globs of glue at the end of each finger is all that is left of those glamorous nails.

"Peter, I can't go on anymore."

"You *have* to."

"NO. No more Peter, I don't care how hard they clap and shout, no more, NO MORE."

Good sports or not, these shaky legs of mine cannot support my body anymore. "Peter, I really, really have to go home, I'm sick. Please take me home."

I'm too ill now to care that I didn't dance with Gerry. Gerry, who the last time I caught sight of him was looking quite startled at my deteriorated, disheveled appearance.

Back at home I stumble into my bedroom. How do I get this bloody dress off? I pull, tug and tear at the seam, the seam where there was supposed to be a zip. The material rips and it's off.

In the morning Mom finds both Peter and me with temperatures of 104 and both of us are delirious. My dress, torn and dirty, is in a forlorn heap on the floor. Hugging the floor now, instead of my bosom.

It's another bout of malaria.

SQUAWKING CHICKEN NECK

The bar is especially dark as I enter from the sunlight. Smoke hovers near the ceiling in heavy grey clouds. The chattering and laughter stops abruptly as I walk in. My eyes adjust, and people begin to take shape, some with elbows on the bar, some with drinks halfway to their mouths, all with heads turned in my direction.

There Mom is, sitting on a bar stool next to Leonard Thorne. Billie sways back and forth on her feet on the other side of him, her arm on the counter.

"Look at my daughter's beautiful breasts," Mom announces to the bar, "not like that flat-chested woman her father is seeing. That sour faced bitch would give anything to have my daughter's bosom." I shrivel up inside when she says things like this. She knows I hate it when she draws attention to my too-big boobs, which I consider a curse and an encumbrance.

"*Mom…*"

"Leave your mother alone, she's enjoying herself," Leonard pipes up. He can be so obnoxious.

"That's easy for you to say," I answer him. "You don't have to handle how she gets when she drinks, Leonard. She gets downright nasty."

"Rosebud," Mom says, "You lie like a cheap watch."

"Mom, come on, let's go. I'm not leaving you here."

"Well, it's too bad about you, because I am not leaving. I haven't finished my drink," Mom snaps. Her mean narrow eyes glare at me. Shit!

"Finish then, Mom. You have a heavy day at the salon tomorrow."

"I'll finish when I'm good and ready, and then? Well, then I just may have another drink." She looks at me, her eyes daring me to argue, her mouth tight.

Oh God! When she is in this kind of mood it means trouble. She could take to her bed for a week, or she would pick her hangover up, throw it into the passenger seat of her beat-up, green Volvo, and the three of them would hiccup their way to the liquor store, returning with six pints of Lion Lager. Or worse, she'd take her hangover into the salon and tipple all day, thinking she was fooling her clients. When this happened, I would search for all the alcohol I could find and pour it down the sink.

One time when I thought I had got rid of all the liquor I noticed her eyes narrow with a look of defiance, a look I knew all too well. So when she fell asleep, I went on a search, looking under beds, in drawers, washing baskets, finally lifting the lid off the toilet cistern – Eureka! There, a half bottle of vodka languished. She would not be happy when she woke up and came looking for this bottle.

"Mom, please…."

THUD. I feel the fist in the middle of my back. My knees buckle, and I reach for Leonard's shoulder. What was that?

"You want him? Here, you can have him." Another thud. "You can have him." Billie slurs as she shoves me into Leonard.

My head starts to buzz. I'm filled with a rage I could never imagine having, a rage that surges through me like a speeding train heading for a blank wall, blinding me, except for Billie's throat. Billie's throat I can see. Her scrawny neck fills my vision. It's all I see now in that dingy bar.

I wrap my hands around her throat and squeeze. Squeeze and squeeze. "Let me go," Billie squawks. "Let me go. Let me go." Her eyes bulge out of her head. It registers in my brain that she is terrified. But I cannot stop now. Oh no, I cannot stop. I'm oblivious to the ruckus around me. I hear it, but I do not register that it is because of what *I* am doing.

"What," squeeze, "makes-you-think-I-want-your-old-chinless," squeeze, "husband- you-drunken-old-woman?" I manage two insults, one for her and one for Leonard.

Is that my voice? It can't be, surely. That voice belongs to someone else. Perhaps Marlon Brando in "On the Waterfront."

"Rosebud, let her go, *let her go*! She's drunk. Let go!" Mom's eyes are wide open now. Gone are the slits, as she tries to pry my hands from Billie's throat.

"I-am-going-to-kill-her." Marlon Brando again.

Hands grope me from all directions. Voices lift. "Stop it! Stop it!"

As I am frog-marched out of the bar. I hear Billie blubber. "My Rosemary, you remind me of my Rosemary."

"I am *not* your Rosemary. Not your Rosemary, understand? No wonder your Rosemary won't have anything to do with you," I yell over my shoulder while struggling to get out of the clutches of these two men pulling me, one on each arm, out the bar.

Now Mom comes running after me. So, this is what I have to do when I want to get her out of the darn G&D. Strangle someone. I'm so mad with her.

"Goodness me, Rosebud, you would have strangled her to death."

"I wanted to."

"I have never seen you like that before, darling."

"None of this would have happened had you come when I asked you to, Mom. It's your fault. It's really your fault. And why do you always embarrass me by drawing attention to my boobs. You know I hate it when you do that. I'm sick of pulling you out of that bloody bar Mom."

I'm crying now.

She says nothing for a while. Then, with a little chuckle, "Did you see Billie's face, Rosebud? Did you? She was shocked, shocked. Her eyes were popping out of her head."

"I just saw her neck." I too, chuckle now, coming down from my adrenalin high. "Actually, I did see her eyes. They were standing out on stalks." My chuckle stops. "Mom, please don't talk about my breasts in a bar full of drunks again. Okay?"

"Well, you do have beautiful breasts."

"Mom, I don't want all those drunks looking at my boobs, I don't want anyone looking at my boobs. Don't you understand? I cringe when you say things like that."

"Okay, okay I won't do it again."

"You always say that, Mom, until the next time."

"I mean it this time."

We continue in silence for a while and then I start laughing. "Poor old Billie. Perhaps she thought I was you, Mom."

I like Billie. Really, I do. She is very funny, especially when she speaks in gobble-de-gook language. She is extremely clever at making up words. Billie is not an attractive woman, though she may have been at one time. She is very thin with a blotchy face, no chin to speak of and a beak for a nose. I can't make up my mind whether she reminds me of a chicken or tortoise, especially in profile. She squawked like a chicken when I had her by the neck tonight. Billie walks with the tottering gait alcoholics perfect to keep themselves vertical.

Though Leonard himself had had Billie blacklisted from all the pubs in town, I am sure he wants to hasten her demise. I witnessed an incident where he asked her what she wanted to drink, and she replied, "Nothing thank you, I'm on the wagon." He walked up to the bar, ordered her a whiskey and milk, which he placed on the table in front of her. And she, of course, drank it.

Whenever Leonard had a big court case, though, Billie would stop drinking and attend every part of the trial. She tried, poor thing, as Mom would say. I feel quite bad about nearly strangling her, even though she deserved it. Punching me in the back like that. She is a very sick lady, beyond all help. Billie died a few years after that incident, from alcohol poisoning. She had open sores you could put a fist in.

No one was surprised.

THE BULLFIGHT

Mom perms my hair and dyes it auburn. "It looks terrible," I say.

Mom says, "No it doesn't, you look beautiful."

"NO, I don't, I look like a freak!"

"It will relax, Rosebud."

"Well, I'm not going anywhere until it does," I say close to tears, tugging at the frizz.

Looking down on the street Mom spies George Trataris in his shiny new red convertible and she calls out to him, "Yoohoo, George. Why don't you take Rosebud for a drive in your new car?"

Shrinking in my seat I say, "No, no, no, Mom, I don't want to go for a drive."

"Hello Pamela," George shouts up at her. "How about tomorrow? Some friends and I are going over the border. Rosebud can join us. I'll pick her up at ten a.m. if that's okay."

"Okay," says Mom, "She'll be ready."

I'm so embarrassed, "How could you do that Mom? I told you I'm not going anywhere with this frizzy hair. Besides, how can you just invite me to go with him? It's embarrassing, Mom. George is way too polite to say no."

"Oh, come on Rosebud, George is dying to take you out. Let's wash your hair again and set it in large rollers." My hair does look better but I'm still not very happy about the arrangement and I could kick myself for not saying I didn't want to go.

The next morning as I am about to walk out the door Mom stops me to pinch my cheeks and put some lipstick on me. The offering is ready!

Ten of us drive over to this remote Portuguese East African outpost seeking piri-pii prawns and Prego's (garlic steak in famously fabulous Portuguese yeasty rolls.) We had driven in two cars. After lunch, we strolled around the dusty little town and joined a crowd heading into a bullfight. We settle down on a high bench and wait, not knowing what to expect from this bullfight.

The gates burst open to cheers of: Ole! Ole!

Dust clouds swirl as five, bone-protruding-skinny, wild eyed, dung-squirting bulls skid and thrash into, then about, the arena to much laughing and cheering from the crowd.

More cheers as a hodgepodge of matadors race in, waving and bowing to the crowd. No beautifully embroidered boleros, no red capes. Their attire consists of dirty, scruffy, shorts and shirts.

"If you were expecting glamour here today, you're not going to get it, I'm afraid," announces George Trataris, the spoilt playboy as mom calls him.

It's hard to tell whether the bulls are more afraid of the matadors, or the other way around, as each spends the entire time running away from the other in confusion. When the bulls and matadors do occasionally bump into each other, by mistake, it causes both to turn and run in opposite directions, in panic. This brings on more raucous laughter from the benches.

Matadors leap and scramble over the fence into a safety corridor if they think a bull is coming at them. Meanwhile the poor thing is just running by with its diarrhea. More roars of laughter from the spectators.

It's getting late, so we have to leave and race back to the border post before it closes or else we will be stuck here for the night. None of us want to do that. Piling into the cars, out of order from our entry, we get to the border just in time.

George is in his convertible with the roof down. I drove over with George, but I'm going back in the other car. George is ahead and is the first at the gate. He stops, shows papers to the guard. Nods, waves his arms around, laughs.

"Whoa! Did you see that?" someone in our car shouts.

"What?"

"The border guard just hit George with his baton."

"What?"

"He hit him! Hit him with his baton. Now he's running back to his guardhouse."

Uh-oh.

George's tires spin, dust and stones fly, his car skids and crashes through the barrier. We follow, right on his tail lights as the guard reappears with a shotgun.

Bang, bang, bang.

"My God, he is firing at us," someone screams. "DUCK!"

"Hurry, hurry!"

We make our escape unscathed, except for George, who has a bump on his head and is now parked outside a trading store. "Stop, there's George! Let's get cokes."

"What happened, George? Didn't he like your face?" Ha! Ha!

"Ach man, you know how excitable these Portuguese are. He was confused because we were in different cars, and the papers he had didn't match the passengers to the car. I tried to joke with him, I told him the others liked his country so much they decided to stay. He got really, really mad and I laughed. He didn't like that."

"Really, George, don't mess with the Portuguese, especially those with guns, man," says Gerry.

We were lucky. We dodged a bullet, or two!

I doubt if any of us will be going back there, especially not to see a bullfight. Anyway, you can get better piri-piri prawns and Prego's at the Flamingo Restaurant or the Portuguese Hotel, in Blantyre.

I don't hear from George again. He knows a coloured is not supposed to date a white girl.

There is not much for a teenager to do in Nyasaland. We create our own entertainment. Television is unheard of. It was not unusual to drive fifty miles for a house party on a tea estate. And of course, there is the Lake Nyasa and Mulanji Mountain. There is a cinema too, the Rainbow Theatre, the only theatre, at least as far as I knew.

At the end of every film one is expected to stand for "God Save the Queen." Of course, there is always a mad dash for the exit while the anthem is playing. Only a few loyalist diehards remain standing until the very end.

Someone has the bright idea to quash this behavior by playing "God Save the Queen" before the movie begins. This worked for a while, until the irreverent crowd figured out that they could arrive a bit later. "We don't have to rush you know – they play that bloody anthem first."

Chase a Crooked Shadow is a scary film playing at the Rainbow. If one happens to be driving past the theatre at a certain time, you hear a collective scream emitting from the building. I hear that scream and I'm curious, so I go to the film with Sally.

It's a particular part that does it. Bad guys are trying to drive the protagonist mad. She is standing in a room where she is being kept hostage and thinks she is alone. She turns and jumps in fright when she sees the stone-faced woman behind her. The theatre screams, I scream, everyone screams. A woman baddie is standing behind her silently holding a tray with a drink on it. They stare at each other, the baddie and the hostage. Everyone knows there is a drug in that drink.

Don't take that drink don't take that drink don't take that drink, I find myself silently chanting. In the hush of this tense moment a young man at the back of the theatre jumps out of his seat and yells. "WHO ARE YOU AND WHY?"

Everyone jumps again with this second fright. Then there is a loud roar as the whole theatre laughs. No one can take this film seriously now.

On the way to the Rainbow there is a notorious section called the "red light district." Of course there are no red lights, or for that matter, no lights of any colour.

Dad would say that if your car happened to break down on that road, as cars are prone to do with frequency in Nyasaland, you should get out and push it out of sight, especially if you are a white male on your own. Being a "well-travelled" road, rumors travelled well too. "You know he fraternizes with black prostitutes, don't you?"

"No, I didn't, how do you know that?"

"His car was seen on that road last night. Why else would his car be there?"

"Who would have thought it? You just never know."

I never went to the Rainbow Theatre again, or, for that matter across the border to that Portuguese outpost.

Teenagers are abuzz. There is a new boy in town.

Mom says I have nine lives, like a cat. I had used up three, blue baby, polio and malaria, and was about to use another.

THE CRASH AND
A RUINED LEG

He takes me for a ride on his motorcycle, reaching speeds of 80 and 90 mph. It's so exciting, exhilarating. I love it. Even though I'm a little scared, I want to do it again. His name is Peter Massey and he's from the "big" city of Salisbury.

After the ride, I notice huge raised bumps all over Peter's arms and face, like giant goose bumps. "What's that?" I say, pointing to his arms.

He looks down. "Withdrawals."

"Withdrawals? From what?"

"Drugs."

"Drugs?"

I'm an echo.

"Yeah, that's why I'm here, in Nyasaland."

"Oh."

"Yeah, my parents sent me here to get away from my friends."

"Oh." That echo again.

Wow. No one I have ever heard of did drugs. Peter Massey is immediately elevated to a place of mystery and awe. Better not tell anyone about this.

I never get on Peter Massey's motorbike again, but I did get into an old rattletrap Studebaker with him and three friends of his. We are driving up to the Lake, the whole gang, Peter, Gary, Lynn and me, in Gary's Stud, as he called it.

"Look out!" someone screamed. Perhaps it was me? Instinctively I pull my right foot up and shield my face with my leg and arms, as a car hurtles out of a side road and hits the Stud on my side. The scrunch of metal on metal is earsplitting. The passenger seat moves back, with the impact slamming into my foot. The silence that follows is deafening, or was it my ears? Had they stopped hearing? Had they?

The tingling that started in my head moves down through my body to my feet. Silence.

One minute? Five minutes? Thirty minutes?

Then noise and clamour erupts as I am carried into a house. Is this a dream? The tingling won't stop but my ears are listening now as someone says, "Is she okay?"

"I don't know." It's Peter and tears are running down his cheeks. Why is he crying?

"Look at it, look at her leg. She needs to go to the hospital," says a strange voice.

"My foot, my foot, be careful, it hurts, be careful," I cry as hands and bodies take me outside. I'm the only one really hurt. I am placed in the back seat of a car and taken to Zomba Hospital. Peter tells the doctor that I was ashen-faced, had a glazed look in my eyes and seemed not to be able to hear. "I can hear now," I pipe in.

Shock, the Doctor says.

I'm shocked now as I watch my leg swell at an alarming rate. The tingling has left. The pain has arrived, so much pain I can hardly bear it.

"Your ligaments are torn, and a rather large round piece of bone has chipped off your ankle. We'll have to leave it there I'm afraid."

I'm the one afraid; afraid the good doctor doesn't know what he's doing. He is so young. Is he even a doctor?

They encase my leg from knee to foot in a plaster cast and instruct me to return in six weeks to have the cast removed. It's been hours since I left home and of course the lake trip is abandoned. I know I have to go home and tell Mom about this.

"What happened to the people in the other car? Were they hurt?" I ask Gary on the drive home.

"Ach man, you know munts, they think there is only one car on the road and it's the one that has already passed them. No, they weren't hurt. I feel like hurting them though. My car's buggered, man," Gary complains. "And of course, they don't have insurance."

"Do you? Have insurance that is?"

"No, of course not."

"Whose car is this we're in?"

"I borrowed it to take you to the hospital."

Two weeks later the loose cast chaffs my calves. The darn itching is driving me bananas. I hack away at the plaster with a knife and scissors. "Rosebud, what are you doing?" Mom asks.

"Taking this cast off."

"Why? Shouldn't you let the hospital do that?"

"Nooo. They don't know what they're doing at that Zomba Hospital."

"And you do?"

"All I know is that the swelling has gone down, and this cast is too big now. It's chaffing my leg and driving me mad, Mom."

I finally get it off.

"Look at your leg, Rosebud," Mom says, bursting into tears.

I'm looking at my leg and it doesn't look good. Will it ever look okay?

"Mom, don't cry, don't cry it's okay. I'll just wear trousers."

"It's not funny, Rosebud. Your leg is ruined."

It is ruined. I want to cry, but I don't. I laugh even though I don't think it's funny. There I go again. Laughing when I should be crying. But what can I do about it? Nothing. There is nothing I can do about this ugly, crippled leg.

"I could stand and beg on the street corner, Mom. Help you pay for your hairdryers." Mom is not amused.

From the ankle to the knee there are large glassy blisters. The calf is at least three inches thinner than the calf on my right leg and it's black and purple. The thinness, I learn later, is from the ligaments atrophying.

Though my right leg is a mess, I know I am extremely lucky. It could have been a lot worse.

Of course, there was to be no more motorbike riding while my leg was in a cast. Now that the cast is gone, so is Peter, summoned back to Salisbury, for some unknown or unremembered reason.

LAKE NYASA AND BUSH TELEGRAPH

Lake Nyasa is a popular place to get away to and most people do just that every chance they got. It is one of the most beautiful lakes in Africa. Three hundred and sixty-five miles long and fifty-two miles wide, it's said the lake is fed by an underground spring from the Shire River, the river Peter hunts crocodiles on. Chambo, a fresh water bream, are so abundant in its waters, it's a staple diet throughout the land. Sunsets and sunrises are spectacular. On a clear day, one can see Tanganyika on the opposite side.

What I love most, what stirs me the most, is the hauntingly beautiful cry of the fish eagle. Their cries echo around the lake, as they swoop and snatch fish. They're an awe-inspiring sight with their huge wing-span as they rise with a flashing silver fish in their talons.

Crocodiles and hippos are always a danger to be aware of. Both kill many natives, especially those who make a habit of returning to the same spot over a period of time, to wash their clothes in the lake. The lake can be as treacherous as it is beautiful. Storms occur with little notice, whipping up waves ten feet high in the blink of an eye.

Mom and Peter rented a cottage at Monkey Bay for the weekend, to get away from ex-boxer Joe Darrach for a while. They managed to get a lift to the lake, as Mom no longer had a car. Peter would later confess that he and Mom had had a piss-up at the hotel bar. While walking along the beach back to their cottage, Mom stood on a puff adder. It was after midnight and because they were both inebriated, they did not give the bite the attention it warranted.

In the early hours of the morning Mom was running a high fever and her foot was the size of a football. Red lines ran up her leg to her groin. Very alarmed, Peter was desperately trying to find some-one at the hotel to take him and Mom to the hospital in Lilongwe. This proved to be an impossible quest, given the early hour, so he put the word out amongst the black staff, the only ones up at that hour, that Mom had been bitten by a puff adder and needed to go to the hospital.

It was ten o'clock in the morning when the knock came to their cottage door. Peter opened the door to find a witchdoctor standing on the threshold. "I have come to help the Dona. She was bitten by a puff-adder last night," he announced by way of a greeting, "She could die."

That is bush telegraph. It had taken four hours for news to get to the witchdoctor and bring him to this threshold.

"Come in, come in, thank you for coming," Peter says, holding the door open.

Mom said she thought she was going to die. In fact, surely this apparition standing in front of her, with dried, rattling seed pods around his wrists, and blown up animal bladders and hippo teeth hanging around his neck, this apparition with a leopard skin loincloth, surely he was here to deliver her to the other side?

The witchdoctor unwraps a dirty rag. Inside is a large, rolled-up leaf and inside the leaf is a lump of black paste. He brings out a razor blade from a pouch on his waist, takes Moms foot in his hand, makes three incisions on her ankle and two on the top of her foot, then makes two incisions on her good foot. Why the good foot? Only that witchdoctor knows. Besides who are we to question his ancient wisdom? He rubs the black paste into these five cuts.

"The Dona will be getting better now, but you must be taking her to the hospital," he tells Peter as he departs with a couple of Peter's shirts as payment.

Within an hour her fever breaks and Peter finds someone to take him and Mom to the hospital in Lilongwe. "That witchdoctor saved your life, you know," the Doctor tells her. He also tells her that the puff adder is Africa's most dangerous reptile, responsible for more deaths than any other vertebrate. Being sluggish snakes, they generally only bite if you step on them and, of course, that is exactly what she had done the night before. Stepped on the puff adder that was tied to a fisherman's dugout on the beach. The African fishermen do this to discourage thievery. How? I, don't know. This is yet another African mystery.

She was not a thief, at least not of dugouts. Of glasses and ashtrays and robes and such, yes, but not of dugouts.

She would have those black incision scars for the rest of her life, a constant reminder of the dangers, and wonders, of Africa. Mom survived the puff adder but the lake would claim two other victims soon afterwards.

Uncle Sid, Aunt Rose, Stan, (Aunt Rose's son), John, (a friend of Stan's), Cleone and Dad were vacationing together at one of the lake resorts. Uncle Sid would often proclaim that he knew the lake *like the back of his hand*. He had fished that lake for over 30 years.

Uncle Sid, Stan and John decide to take the boat out fishing. It's a gorgeous day. The sun shimmering on the water beckons them.

As they're preparing to launch the boat, an old, black, local fisherman approaches Uncle Sid. "Bwana Bell, it's not good today for fishing."

Surprised, Uncle Sid asks. "Why not, Bambo? It's a beautiful day."

"Please, Bwana, the lake is not happy today."

"Oh, don't worry Bambo, we will be fine."

They're two miles out when the storm hits. Black clouds appear from nowhere and gale force winds whip up white horses on the water. Rain pounds the beach.

The boat is nowhere to be seen. Initially, though somewhat uneasy, no one was too worried. After all, Uncle Sid knows the lake like the back of his hand, doesn't he? And Stan was extremely fit, an excellent swimmer.

After a while, when there is still no sign of the boat, search parties are summoned. But the lake is too rough to go out on. People stand on the beach, bombarded by the rain and wind, scanning the horizon. Hours later John, the least fit of the three of them, stumbles onto the shore and collapses. He has swum the couple of miles from where he says the boat capsized. Uncle Sid and Stan never made it.

John had been tossed out one side of the boat and Stan and Uncle Sid the other. It was assumed that perhaps either Uncle Sid or Stan were hit on the head and the other had gone to the rescue. No one will ever know. Their bodies were never found. Had they washed up somewhere, there was a strong possibility they would have been taken by crocodiles.

Around midnight the night watchman summons Dad. "Dona Bell is walking into the lake. The Dona said she wanted to be with her husband and son." Dad managed to get her back to her room where he and Cleone stayed with her.

Uncle Sid thought he knew the lake like the back of his hand and found out too late that he didn't know it at all. Everyone in Nyasaland was shocked at the news of the deaths. Uncle Sid was well-liked and respected.

"It just shows you, one should heed the advice of the old locals. They know the lake better than we do," say voices that echoed around the country.

Lake cottage.

CHAOS ON THE ROADS

Some friends, Sally, Gerry, Larry, Doreen, Aunt Patty and I, have spent the weekend at Palm Beach, Lake Nyasa, and it's time to pack up and head home. We came up in two cars, three to a car. It's about a six-hour drive back to Blantyre due to the bad strip roads (2 parallel tarmac strips, approximately 2 feet wide and 5 inches high, the width of a car apart for your tyres to travel on. One has to move off the strips to allow an oncoming car to pass, this can be hard on your tyres.) and all other manner of obstacles one encounters on roads in Africa.

It's always chaos. There are goats, dogs, chickens, blaring hooters, wobbling bicyclists, bicycles piled high with chickens in mesh baskets and bundles of goodness only knows what else, tied onto carriers. Towers of stuff, precariously swaying with each pedal and more often than not, a passenger sitting side-saddle on the crossbar. It's a common, comic sight, to see this lot fall, every now and then, by the wayside, having slipped off the tarmac strip.

"Hey Rosebud, last night you said you wish someone would teach you to drive. I will." Larry offers.

"You will?"

"Yes. You can drive my Jeep back."

"Really? Thanks, Larry." Larry, a nice guy, is a friend of Stan's, Aunt Rose's son. He is very stiff and proper in his khaki shirt, long shorts and knee-high socks. Pukka English.

"Anyone want to come with us?" Larry asks.

"No, you guys go on your own." Aunt Patty, Sally, Gerry and Doreen reply in unison.

"Huh! Sissies," I say.

"Okay, this is the gear stick. You take off in first gear, then change to second, then third, and when you have enough speed you change to fourth."

"Okay, what is this gear?"

"Don't worry about that, it's over-drive. We won't need it."

"This is the brake pedal, this is the clutch. You push that down, hold it down while you change gear, then slowly release it while accelerating, okay?"

"Okay."

"That is the accelerator."

"Okay. Like this?"

"Yes."

Clutch down, gear in, accelerate, clutch out, the Jeep lurches forward alarmingly, like a mad buffalo, shudders, shakes and stops dead as my foot hits the brake. Larry is almost thrown through the windscreen.

"Jesus, Rosemary. Let the clutch out SLOWLY, at the same time put your foot down on the accelerator, SLOWLY."

"I'm sorry."

"It's okay, you're learning."

"Like this?"

"Yes, yes – that's good, now change into second, gently, that's good, now change to third."

GRIIIIND.

What the hell!...*what* is that jaw clenching, gut wrenching, ear splitting, screeeech?

CLUNK. CLUNK....

"Jesus, STOP."

"What did I do?"

"You didn't push the bloody clutch in."

"Well, you don't have to scream at me."

"I'm sorry. Move over and I'll show you."

"You drive."

"No, you are going to drive. Watch me." Slowly he goes through the gears. "Got it?"

"Yes, I think so."

"Why are you shaking?"

"Because it's scary Larry. There's too much to do at the same time."

"You'll get it, come on."

I get it and we are on our way.

"I hate these strips, Larry."

"I know, just keep all four wheels on them. They chew your tyres up if you slip off."

"What if a car comes the other way?"

"Well of course, then you have to pull off them, hold the steering wheel tight and keep your two right tyres on the left strip."

"Okay."

"You are doing well."

"Car coming, Car coming."

"Don't panic. Pull over. PULL OVER – NOW!"

CADUNK. Stones fly, clunk, ping, ping on the under belly of this Jeep that is a bucking buffalo again. Hoot, hoot, comes the sound of a horn. Did that man shake his fist at me?

Larry holds onto the roll bar with both hands, his knuckles white, his face drained of all colour.

I giggle. Why do I always giggle when I'm nervous?

"It's not bloody funny."

"I think it's rather funny."

"WATCH OUT – goats. GOATS!"

Swerve. Thunk. Thunk. Off the bloody strips again.

"I *saw* them, Larry."

"No, you didn't."

"YES. I. DID."

"Don't look at me, look at the road."

"I *am* looking at the road."

"You are NOT, you're looking at me, Watch out. Watch out for that woman."

"What WOMAN?"

"That woman selling bloody mangoes on…, oh shit… TOO late."

"AYEeeeeeee."

That-woman flees into the bush, arms flaying. The wheels, the ones off the strip, plough over her mangoes lined up on a blanket.

I'm way too busy to care. Larry has both hands on the roll bar again. Perhaps he never took them off? Head turned backwards. "Jesus Christ, Rosemary, you just missed her."

"Don't talk to me. I'm trying to get back on these damn strips."

"Slow down, slow DOWN."

"Shut up, who's driving this car, you or me?"

"You, unfortunately."

I'm beginning to dislike Larry.

"You could have killed that woman." Rubbing it in now.

"Why do they have to put their bloody mangoes so close to the road."

"That's no reason to try and kill her."

"Oh," chuckle, "I thought it was. Larry, you're as white as a ghost."

"Don't LOOK AT ME."

"CAR COMING."

With a jerk of the steering wheel I pull off, both strips. Now we're bouncing, bucking really, and I hold on to that wheel for all I'm worth, teeth rattling. Skid, bump, bump, over ruts, slam the brakes, slide, stones like missiles pinging off the Jeep. Chickens, dogs, goats fly, flee, clucking, yelping, baaing. Pandemonium abounds.

The buffalo shudders, snorts and stops – miraculously it stops – just short of more women and mangoes and screaming potbellied picanins. Startled, bulging eyed mothers and their snotty-nosed children, dust layering their faces and hair, turning black to tan. Brightly coloured sarongs and mismatched blouses, in disarray, approach through the cloud of dust with small steps, to this galimoto that so rudely landed among them and their mangoes.

We sit. Sit still and quiet, while dust runs down the windscreen in ripples.

Faces with big grins, grins showing whiter than white teeth, materialize through the dust, around the car. Dear little picanins, undaunted by this close catastrophe, hold out their hands for sweets, of which we have none. But we buy mangoes, penny a dozen, and give them all our loose change.

"You drive now," I say.

"Okay." A very rapid, very eager, move over NOW, okay.

With an undignified pout I stare out the side window.

"It's not your fault…it was a bad idea to try and teach you to drive on this terrible road."

Don't its-not-your-fault-me, I think to myself, not done with pouting yet.

"We'll do it again on a decent road."

"Decent road? There are no decent roads in this country."

He smiles. "At least there were no elephants crossing the road."

"Yeah." I smile back. "That would have been something, Elephant versus Buffalo."

I get my driver's license a month later. But I don't have a car to drive so it languishes in my handbag. I take it out every now and then to stare at it with a feeling of accomplishment.

Relaxing at the Lake. Aunty Pat on
the left and me on the right.

ACCEPTANCE

Acceptance happened gradually as I got older. I accepted that Dad had another life, another family and that he was happy. Cleone catered to his every need. She respected him, and when he got home after work she was there to greet him. There were no scenes, no drama. His life was, for the most part, peaceful now.

When I was younger the loss of him, physically, emotionally and biologically, was a constant ache in my heart. He and I never discussed my dubious parentage. For one thing I was by then a master at suppressing painful subjects. Secondly talking to him about it would have made it real. Better for there to be doubt, better that he think that I think he is my real father. There is that miniscule chance that he could think I *am* his real daughter.

The burden I had carried since meeting Fish Fingers slowly receded, mainly due to the fact that Dad never treated me differently than my siblings. But the "loss" of him in our day-to-day lives left me feeling cheated. It would take many, many years for me to come to truly believe that Dad didn't care whether Peter and I were his biological children. He had a generous heart.

Dad holding me as a baby. Look at his
smile. He seems quite happy with me.

CROCODILES AND WAVING SIGNS

I don't see much of Dad, he lives eight miles out of Limbe and I live in Blantyre. He will occasionally pop into the Salon when he has errands in Blantyre, mainly to see Avril and me. On these occasions, Mom would disappear into one of the cubicles, brush her hair, pinch her cheeks and refresh her lipstick, emerging as this sultry siren with sucked-in cheeks trying so hard to captivate Dad. These visits would be brief but pleasant, as long as the Bells weren't mentioned. Peter has maintained a good relationship with Cleone and Aunt Rose, and is staying with them while he tries to establish a sign-writing business.

One day Dad calls me at the salon. "Rosebud," he, says, "could you please finish a sign that Peter started for Mr. Patel's store? Peter started it months ago. Mr. Patel paid him half, but Peter never finished the job. Goodness knows where he is. Patel will pay you the other half for the job if you'll do it."

Mr. Patel owns a trading store halfway between Limbe and Blantyre. So, he paid Peter half and Peter gave him half, didn't he? Don't they say you get what you pay for?

"Okay Dad, but I'm not as good as Peter. He's the sign writer, I'm not,"

"That's okay, Rosebud. At least Patel will have a sign. Then perhaps he will stop bothering me."

So, I go on and finish the sign and I get paid my half and it looks good, really. I managed to match Peter's lettering. I drive past Mr. Patel's store all the time just to see how good it looks. Mr. Patel is very happy.

Then the rains come.

Rain, chiperone, rain, chiperone, every day, for weeks. The sign swells and curls at the edges. The chipboard Peter had used soaks up the water like a sponge, until the veneer separates from the board.

When I drive by, the veneer covering the part that said, Patel's Trading Store, painted on it in red lettering, is shaded with black. Shaded with doom. The part that now dangles down from the board, waving at me. Is it waving for help? Or is it waving good-bye? I stop driving by the store. It's too uncomfortable.

Dad gives Mr. Patel his money back. Perhaps Peter intended to put a waterproof edging on that board. I don't know. All I knew was that Peter had moved on to bigger things, with not a thought of Mr. Patel and his waving sign. Crocodile hunting! Crocodiles and their soft underbelly used to make shoes and handbags, is where the money is now, he thinks. He says he's going to make tons of money, he and Marney Stein.

Peter met Marney Stein at the Blantyre Club. Marney, a crocodile hunter from Northern Rhodesia, had been hunting on the Zambezi River for a few years, but heard that crocs were abundant on the

Shire River, in Nyasaland, south of Lewonde Ferry. Marney needed a partner. Crocodile hunting is not something you can do alone.

Peter knew the area. He also knew a good thing when it slapped him in the face. Marney and Peter formed a partnership and set about the business of crocodile hunting. Licenses were hard to get but they were able to operate under the license of a recently retired hunter, Peter Gurney. They negotiated an agreement to use Gurney's tug and hunting boat, aptly named the Rusty Can. They hired Gurney's experienced local helper, known as Boat Boy.

Stocking up on supplies, they set off to meet the numerous chiefs along the forty-odd mile stretch of river they would be covering. Selecting four or five villages along the course of the hunt, they rented a hut with ground area for curing their catch, in each village.

The chiefs of the villages they chose welcomed them with open arms, kaffir beer and palm wine. They were happy to have the crocs killed since a number of women and children had disappeared during the course of a year, while washing or swimming at the river. The money they would be paid was welcome as well.

"You can't be a sissy, for this game," Peter says. It's grueling, perilous work, entailing a week of hunting followed by a week of recuperating from the exhaustion, the septic sores caused by leeches and bouts of six-o'clock fever. Most people who had had malaria often got the same symptoms as the sun went down. Malaria was a constant lurking danger from the thick cloud of mosquitos buzzing around one's head from dusk to dawn.

Crocodile hunting is night work. On a typical hunt night, Peter and Marney would leave their station in the twenty-foot Rusty Can, towing the tugboat and outboard motor behind them. With searchlights scanning the riverbanks, they'd wait til they saw a croc's eyes. Then they would drop anchor and transfer the hunting equipment onto the tug, leaving Boat Boy with the trusty Primas stove, on the Rusty Can to keep coffee and brandy at the ready.

Crocs hug the riverbanks at night, their snouts like floating driftwood. Mesmerized by the searchlight, their eyes shine like beacons, allowing a perfect target for a brain shot. Cut the motor, drift up to within a foot of the crocodile, aim. BANG.

A good shot between the eyes sinks a croc rapidly. Two minutes is all the time you have to jump into the river and rope them, tie them alongside the tug, leap back into the boat. If by chance you delivered a foul shot, this is even more dangerous, as the croc must be wrestled to get the rope around its body, while you avoid its lethal tail. The tail could slice you in half, and all this thrashing and splashing about of a wounded croc quickly attracts other crocodiles in the vicinity.

With two crocodiles lashed to the tug, you return to the Rusty Can, where Boat Boy has hot black coffee and the mandatory bottle of brandy to lace it with, plus a lit cigarette to burn the leeches off your body. You can't pull those little bastards off. If you do, their heads remain embedded in your flesh, creating septic sores. When you hold a cigarette to them, they curl and release themselves instantly, leaving a clean hole.

On a number of occasions, when returning to the Rusty Can, Peter and Marney would find Boat

Boy snoring on the bunk with a half empty bottle of brandy at his side. Dumping a bucket of water on him was a short-lived cure. Though he was threatened with being fired, he never was. "Better the devil you know than the one you don't." Peter would say, "Besides the poor little bugger deserves a piss-up now and then. Its tough work."

Now, fortified with coffee and brandy, the crocs are loaded onto the Rusty Can and back Peter and Marney go for another two crocs. This goes on until two or three in the morning. When they have anywhere from six to ten crocs, depending on their size, they would return to their allotted hut. The largest crocodile they shot was sixteen feet long.

Back at the hut, sleep is fitful. The village wakes up just as Peter and Marney put their heads down. The chitter-chatter of picanins at play is a constant noise in the background. By the time they get up, the village chief's skinners had already skinned, staked, and salted the soft underbellies. There the crocs stretch out in the sun to await the hunter's return journey.

After a wash in the river and a meal prepared by Boat Boy, Peter and Marney take off for the next village to repeat this process. Moving from village to village down the mighty Shire River takes about five days. The return trip is very slow, as they work against the current and stop at each village to collect the rolled-up skins and pay the chief.

The average skin was about 864 square inches, and at the going rate of two shillings and sixpence a square inch, the trip, after all expenses were paid, would net them each two thousand pounds. A small fortune then, but a hard way to earn it. The drive back to Blantyre would be a quiet one, with the promise of a hot bath, a good meal and a comfortable bed to sleep in, at the end of it. But first, the smelly skins had to be dropped off with their agent, who would arrange for proper curing.

After four or five hunts, Marney, looking very thin and quite sick, informed Peter that he would have to find a new partner. "I just can't do this anymore Pete." Marney was never seen or heard from again. He may have contracted blackwater fever. That was Peter's guess.

Peter, on the hunt for a new partner, met Andreis DuPlessis, called Dup, one night at the G&D. Peter regaled him with tales of hunting crocodiles and the money to be made from it. Dup was quickly seduced into becoming Peter's new partner. Dup however, only lasted through two hunts before throwing in the towel. "Too tough man, too dangerous," is what he said. Michael, who had accompanied Peter and Marney on a hunt during his school holiday, was safely back at boarding school, so Peter resorted to cajoling his gullible little friend, Gordon Rogers into going with him. Gordon begged out after two days into the hunt, returning to Blantyre. He mumbled about Peter, "He wrestles crocodiles. He jumps in the river full of crocodiles. He's mad, that Peter Fitzgerald. Quite mad."

Having exhausted potential partners, Peter gave up on crocodile hunting, and moved on to the tobacco floors. He, too, avoided driving by Mr. Patel's store where the swollen board still hung, denuded of its hanging veneer now. The sign had nothing to say anymore.

Peter around eighteen years old.

Peter and I looked so alike. Could Sardine man have been his father too?

BWANA BOBBY ADOPTS MONKEY BAY

The young hippopotamus that adopts the shores of Monkey Bay is a small hippo, by hippopotamus standards that is. He only weighs about 5,000 lbs. At the beginning he comes only at night, foraging local vegetable gardens and creating havoc amongst the rows of lettuces and cabbages in the Monkey Bay Hotel's gardens.

Gradually he gets more brazen and starts making daytime appearances. Hannes Muller, the proprietor of the Monkey Bay Hotel is concerned that he would frighten the tourists and harm his business.

"Just throw him cabbages, Bwana," the staff suggests.

So, he does. And it doesn't take long for the hippo to learn that a whistle is followed with a cabbage. Whistle, toss in the open jaw, whistle, toss, becomes a daily routine.

He is named Bwana Bobby. Bwana Bobby gets braver and braver, soon walking amongst the swimmers with his jaws agape, waiting for anything people choose to toss in his mouth, including the odd Lion Ale or Castle Lager. He loved beer!

In no time Bwana Bobby becomes the main attraction at Monkey Bay, attracting more tourists and locals than ever. Guests and visitors have their photographs taken while sitting on his back, or with their heads in his jaws. He is a playful creature and frolics in a lumbering, hippopotamus sort of way, in the water.

"Bwana Bobby has come, get cabbages," tourists shout to waiters. Everyone loves him, but no one more than Geraldine, who spends a lot of time at the lake. She adores him.

Word reached the powers that be (powers that should not have been) that a potentially dangerous situation is developing "up at the lake,'" that a hippo is mingling with tourists.

Oh no!

An indaba is held and it's decided that Bobby should be moved to Blantyre to be housed by the Zoological Society there. An expert who knew about such things is flown up from Salisbury to take care of Bobby's safe transportation and relocation.

No one wants to see Bwana Bobby go and cries of, Fuck the tourists," and "The lake belongs to Bwana Bobby," and "Bobby is a gentle giant," fell on deaf ears. The expert arrives with darts in hand and Bobby is lured into a makeshift crate on the edge of the shore, with cabbages. Once inside, he is darted. As the effects of the injection kick in, Bobby panics, breaks through the pen, staggers into the lake, collapses and drowns.

The Monkey Bay population is stunned – stunned and outraged. Geraldine and Michael are angry and heartbroken over this tragic event. Mom says, "Those bastards need to be shot," a saying of hers that would get her into trouble years later. While living in America, she used it and was almost arrested for a "terrorist threat!'

Bobby receiving a cabbage. Background: Michael sitting on a boat with a big hat on. Top from left: 1. Michael offers Bobby a beer. 2. Michael pouring the beer into Bobby's open mouth. 3. Bobby gets another beer. 4. Frolicking on Bobby's back. 5. Bobby gets another morsel. 6. Bobby waiting for more of anything.

THE UNBURDENING

I'm seventeen or eighteen when I tell Aunt Patty the twisted secret that I have been carrying around with me for eight years. The secret I would go to, push away, go to again. The secret that twisted my head, confused and shamed me. That ugly, shameful thing that had happened in Salisbury, with Henry. That secret just popped out of my mouth with no forethought.

Aunt Patty is very quiet and still when I tell her. Finally she says, "Did you tell Mommy?"

"No. I didn't tell anyone. I felt too ashamed to tell anyone. I don't want you to tell Mom."

"Rosebud, don't cry darling. It wasn't your fault, it really wasn't. You were just a little girl."

She narrows her eyes and spits out, "That bastard. How I wish I could meet him." Aunt Patty had never met Henry, as she lived in Bulawayo at that time, and there wasn't much likelihood that she ever would. He was long gone now.

Eight years gone.

And just like that the burden was lifted and I vowed to put it out of my mind. That space Henry had occupied for so long was emptied, killed, but his ghost lingered. I would tell Mom thirty-five years later. Her reaction was to swing her handbag at my head and call me a liar.

I guess she couldn't accept the responsibility.

REVENGE IS SWEETEST
SERVED COLD

Now, a year later I'm eighteen and contemplating a move to Salisbury.

Mom brought Aunt Patty and her five children up here to Nyasaland, from Gwelo, after the man Aunt Patty had fallen in love with, and with whom she'd had a son, dropped her. He got tired of waiting for Uncle Ernie to give Aunt Patty a divorce, so he found himself another woman.

Now there are eleven living in this flat of Mom's and she is supporting everyone until they find jobs. Aunt Patty flies down to Salisbury to see her solicitor about the ever-elusive divorce, staying a few extra days to visit friends. When she gets back, she takes me into my room, shuts the door and says she has something to tell me.

What? What?

She had arranged to meet her friends, she says, after her appointment with the solicitor at Meikles Hotel. Meikles Hotel is the poshest hotel in Salisbury. I'm all ears, itching to hear whatever this is she has to tell me. Aunt Patty says she and her group of friends are having cocktails in the lounge when they are joined by a couple of men someone in the party knew.

Introductions are made, and more drinks are ordered. One of the newcomers leans towards Aunt Patty. "Did I hear right? Are you Patty Rice?"

"Yes."

"I knew your sister, Pamela. In fact, we were seeing each other for a while, years ago."

"Really? What did you say your name is?"

"Henry."

"Henry?"

"Yes."

"Henry, do you remember Rosemary, Pam's daughter?"

"Oh yes, yes, of course I do"

"Did you give her a sewing machine when she was a little girl?"

"Why, yes. Yes, I did."

"I've waited a long time to meet you, Henry."

"Oh, you have?" Henry beams, flattered, sits up straighter in his chair.

"Yes. I have." With that she swings her handbag, a handbag of sturdy construction always crammed full to overflowing. WHACK! It meets its target, his head! "That's for Rosemary,"

Aunt Patty says, "Rosebud, there was dead silence. I wish you could have seen the startled look on everyone's faces. Their mouths fell open." We are both laughing with glee now.

"What the hell?" he screams, "are you bloody mad, woman?"

"Yes, you bastard!" preparing for another swing, "Bloody mad!" WHACK. Another hit to the head. WHACK, a hit to the shoulder.

"This woman is insane," Henry squeaks, to the table, to curious onlookers stopped in their tracks, to everyone. "Manager!" he yells, "Get the manager. Get the manager!" WHACK. "Get her away from me. Get her away." With his arms shielding his head, he ducks and flees for the exit.

"You know that Meikles has a doorman?" Aunt Patty asks me.

"Yes."

"Well, he is holding the door open, his eyes bulging out of his head, but I'm not finished with the bastard yet, I'm behind him, right behind him and I manage to get one more hit on his back. I whacked him so hard I nearly fell over. I yelled, 'You dirty bastard. That's right, run away.'"

She continued, "When I get back to our table with its stunned occupants, I slap my hands together, sit down, and announce to the wide-eyed audience, 'Let's have another drink. I need to celebrate! I've waited a long time to meet that man, a long time.'"

She takes my hand. "I got him Rosebud, it took a long time, but I got him for you."

By this time, I'm in a heap on the floor, laughing, crying, my knees pulled up to my chin, rolling side to side, "Oh Aunt Patty, thank you, thank you. I wish I could have been there to see his face."

Aunt Patty, dabbing at her eyes, is laughing and crying too, "He got the shock of his life. Yes, I wish you had been there to see the terror in his eyes."

Would I be able to put this thing to rest now? Kill the ghost? Maybe? As Mom would always say, time will tell.

Looking back now, this other person who is-me-now, is so far removed from that incident, so much so that I can look back on it with dispassion. Although I have not, as yet, come to understand just how screwed up I am as far as intimacy and sex is concerned, I feel somewhat vindicated.

Revenge is sweet served cold.

Fighting and screaming and hitting and drinking and drama, drama, drama, was a way of life. I did not understand, not then, about abuse. This ignorance would cost me dearly in the choices I made going forward.

MOVING ON

The departure lounge at Chileka Airport in Blantyre is abuzz with chatter, crying babies, shouted helloes and goodbyes and the clatter of plates in the adjoining canteen. The air is heavy with stale cigarette smoke. Smells of sweaty armpits and unwashed clothes mingle with the canteen smells of coffee, curry, and rancid oil.

"Call me when you get to Salisbury," Mom yells over the hubbub. We are only a few feet apart.

"Of course, Mom," I yell back.

"Pamela, what are you doing here?" It's my brother's friend Griffin.

"Seeing Rosebud off to Salisbury. And you? You need a haircut, young man."

"I know. I didn't have time to make an appointment."

"Sit down," Mom says, digging in her handbag. "I'll give you a quick trim." She retrieves a pair of scissors and proceeds to cut Griffin's hair, right there, contributing to the madness all around us.

Someone in the crowd shouts, "Hey, Pamela, can I be next?"

"No," she smiles "You can make an appointment at the salon."

While Mom snips away, I gaze absentmindedly at a native woman wearing a brightly coloured African sarong tied around her waist and an unbuttoned western blouse, exposing a breast. Europe on top, Africa below. With one enormous, milk-engorged-breast in her hand, she jabs her nipple at her baby's gaping mouth. That baby, having none of it, thrashes its head from side to side in fury. Its screams escalate in volume. I watch the woman with interest now, as her eyes go to the sugar bowl on a table in front of her. Even before she does it, I know what she is going to do. She leans forward, stretching her breast over, down and into the bowl. She dips her nipple into the sugar, swirls it around to get the nipple fully coated, then pops it into the baby's yawning mouth mid-scream. The baby's eyes widen in surprise for just a moment, then it suckles lustily, fat little cheeks going in and out. Aaah.

I look over at another scene, my mother, who is laughing and chatting to people around her. This always happens; she draws people to her like a magnet. My wild, fierce, incorrigible, mother, my mother – a saviour and destroyer.

My heart tugs. I feel both excitement and trepidation about going to the big city of Salisbury. What awaits me there? Will I be able to find a job, a place to stay? Is this the right move? I have a few hundred Rhodesian dollars in my pocket, but I know Mom will send more if I need it, even if it means those hairdryers will have to rock-n-roll down the hill again. My checked-in baggage is light but all this other baggage I carry inside me, the baggage without handles, is heavy and cumbersome.

Suddenly Mom looks so vulnerable. I wonder why she stays with these men that beat her. Perhaps she is looking for someone like her father? She would often say, "Harry Richmond, my Daddy, was a *real* man." Was that her measure of a man, a real man? One who beats his wife, as he did? Would she have stayed with my Dad if he had hit her? *I will never stay with a man who beats me.* I make this promise to myself in total ignorance. It will be years before I would come to understand that words can be far worse weapons than fists, that some words would bombard me, erode me, the inside of me, leaving scars undetected by the naked eye.

I'm sad waiting here at Chileka Airport, sad and worried. Sad, because I am leaving my adored little sister, Avril, who is ten years old. I worry about who will watch out for both her and Mom. Who will protect them from Irish Joe? And who will protect Avril from Mom? I think back to the time a few years ago when Avril discovered her pet white mouse had given birth to a number of babies. She was so excited she carried the shoebox they were in to show Mom. Mom, who had a tankard of beer in her hand, picked the tiny bald pink babies up by their tails and much to Avrils' distress, drowned them, one by one, in her beer. Now, looking back at that cruel incident, I'm mad at her. That's what it's like with Mom. Conflicting emotions race around my chest so fast, I feel panicky.

The last call for boarding my flight is announced. I rush over to Mom, the baby mouse killer, hug her hard. I tell her I love her, bundle up all my insecurities, fears and notions of romance and make my way to the plane with an ache in my heart. Half way up the gangway, I turn. My eyes seek out and find Mom waving wildly. She is shouting something. I can't hear her over the noise of the engine. I wave, she waves. I blow her a kiss as people brush past me. She blows a kiss back to me.

This picture of me was taken just after my arrival in Salisbury

PICTURES

Harry Walker Richmond

Top Left: Muriel and
Flora Richmond (my grandmother)
Bottom left: Sheba, Patricia and
Pamela (my mother)

Mom at 17

Mom and Peter in Filabuzi

Me with my nurse doll

Geraldine, Mom, me and Avril

Aunt Patty and Mom when we
visited Aunt Patty on the farm

Mick (Michael) in Nyasaland 1955

Mom in the black taffeta dress
she made herself. 1939

Uncle Ernie (Rumble Bum)

Mom in the courtyard outside her salon 1955

Leonard Thorne in court, on the right.
Mom would marry Leonard a few
years after I left Nyasaland.